ADVANCE PRAISE FOR *ARAMCO BRAT*

"A quality investment organization needs intelligent professionals that bring a diversity of insights to its decision making. It's hard to imagine an upbringing more unusual and challenging than that experienced by Rich. He was an excellent securities analyst, an excellent portfolio manager, a unique person with a unique story."

—GEORGE COLLINS, former Chief Executive Officer, T. Rowe Price Group

"Rich Howard became a charter member of the National Association of Petroleum Investment Analysts in 1973. Over the past 48 years he has often shared his industry knowledge, but never the story of how that wisdom was acquired. In *Aramco Brat* we learn of one youth's not-so-easy path toward a professional investing career."

—NANCY PRUE, Director and former President, NAPIA, and former President of Petroleum and Resources Corporation

"We did not live these stories, but they are a big part of our lives. As we grew up, Rich Howard (aka Dad), shared with us his youthful adventures—the pleasant ones anyway—and we were always ready to listen. With this book, Dad's voice and love will live on for our children, their children to come, and all Brats."

—ROBERT and PAUL HOWARD

ARAMCO BRAT

ARAMCO BRAT

HOW ARABIA, OIL, GOLD, AND TRAGEDY SHAPED MY LIFE

RICHARD P. HOWARD

Copyright © 2021 Richard P. Howard

ISBN: 979-8-9852272-0-8

All rights reserved. No part of this publication may be reproduced, distributed, or transmitted in any form or by any means, including photocopying, recording, or other electronic or mechanical methods, without the prior written permission of the publisher, except in the case of brief quotations embodied in critical reviews and certain other noncommercial uses permitted by copyright law. For permission requests, contact aramcobratbook@gmail.com.

Cover and interior design by *the*BookDesigners

Printed in the United States

First Edition

*This book is dedicated to:
My family—past, present, and future; the many
diverse members of the Saudi Aramco Community;
and the wonderful people of Saudi Arabia—
may all know their history.*

Let us therefore brace ourselves to our duties and so bear ourselves that if the British Empire and its Commonwealth last for a thousand years, men will still say, "This was their finest hour."

—Winston Churchill, June 18, 1940

TABLE OF CONTENTS

Introduction *1*

Chapter 1: The Crash 3
Chapter 2: Nomadic Youth 9
Chapter 3: "May God Give You Strength" 19
Chapter 4: Dhahran and Its School 27
Chapter 5: Khobar Kid 34
Chapter 6: Crusader Castles 45
Chapter 7: The Dhahran—RT Road 51
Chapter 8: Boiling Point 57
Chapter 9: Before Bratdom 67
Chapter 10: Vacation Memories 77
Chapter 11: Howard Family Aramco Deities 84
Chapter 12: Home Ownership 90
Chapter 13: The Theater Beckons 101
Chapter 14: School, Sports, and Scouts 106
Chapter 15: Spies and Villains 116
Chapter 16: Randolph Meriwether Vaughan 122
Chapter 17: Golden Speculation 129
Chapter 18: Cranbrook School 136
Chapter 19: Summer of '64 143
Chapter 20: After the Crash 152
Chapter 21: An Agent in Place 160
Chapter 22: Reflections 164

Acknowledgments *175*
About the Author *177*

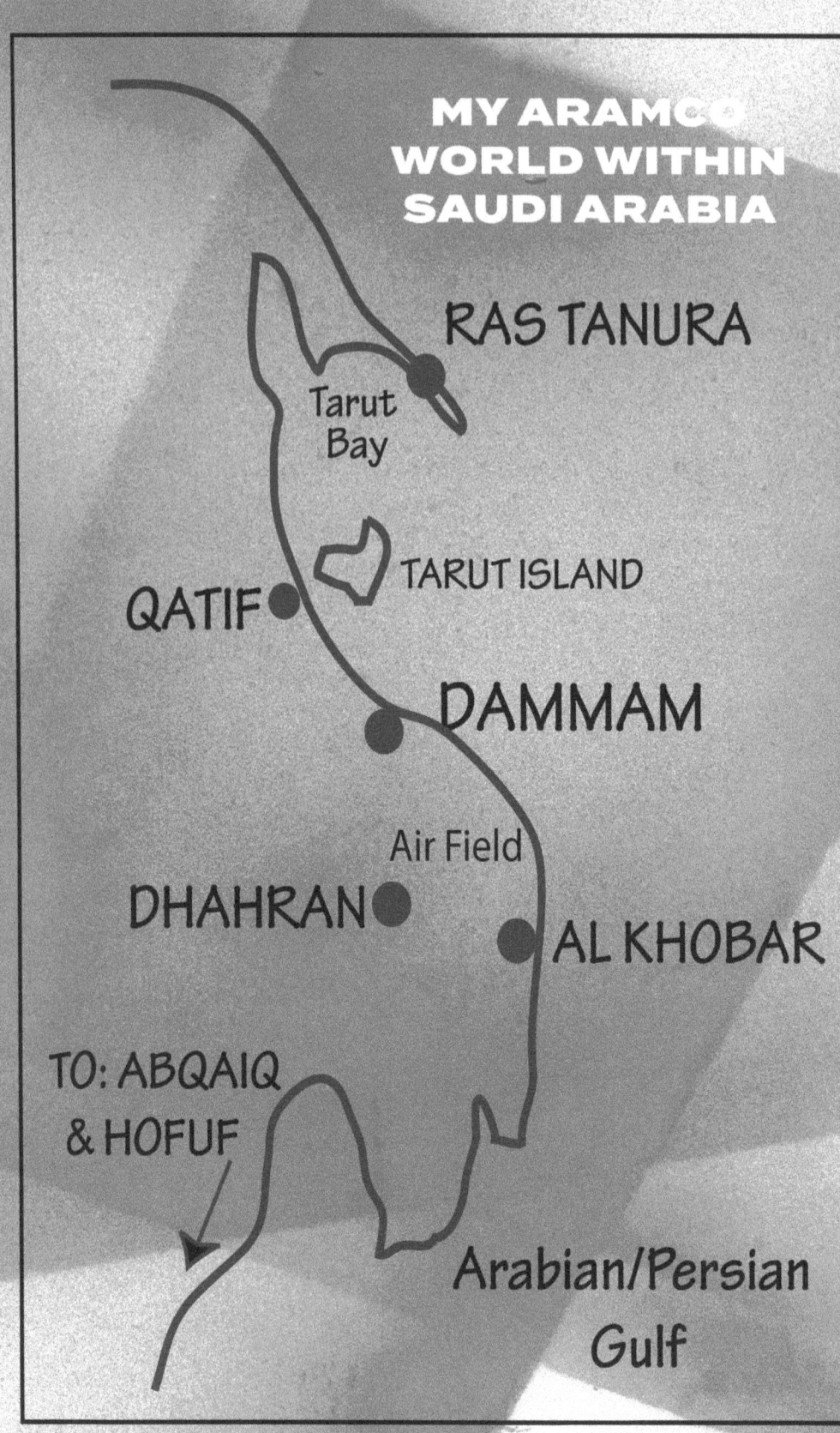

INTRODUCTION

Aramco Brat is not a novel. Fiction follows themes, builds toward a climax, and generally makes sense. In comparison, this memoir is a very messy collection of observations, experiences, and a perhaps 90 percent certain conclusion. Some will accept it uncritically while some will reject it categorically; most will find plausibility. The book is largely set in the Middle East over the dozen years beginning in 1954. A lot changed in this region during those years, and much more has since. One example: the Arabian Peninsula then contained thirteen political entities, eleven clearly dominated by the British Empire and all insignificant in the broader world. At that time only centrally located Saudi Arabia, by far the largest entity, and mountainous Yemen could be considered independent, and neither were considered important by most Americans (Saudi Arabia's population was perhaps three million town dwellers and a half-million uncountable nomads at the time).

By 1965, Great Britain's influence in the region was but a shadow, while today only a memory. With the creation of the United Arab Emirates and the absorption of Aden into Yemen, there are now only six countries on the peninsula, but what a change in their status. Oil and natural gas production and the money it generates turned four of these six into significant players on the world stage. If *Aramco Brat* serves a larger purpose beyond the telling of boyhood adventures and my personal character development, it is as a glimpse into the Arabian world before this dramatic change, a baseline if you will. At the very least there are factual tidbits that deserve being remembered, many to be found in the footnotes.

This book also seeks to be an entertaining story told largely through the eyes of an observant youth. It is not a particularly happy tale—it can't be—but it's not a "downer" either. It is a very different book than those typically set during the period and found on the shelves of bookstores. It is neither scholarly, nor the recollections of a PR type, nor collected tales of youthful highjinks. It is quite simply, to the best of my knowledge, a story littered with truth … I was there. Those readers who shared or studied that world and take exception to my "facts" are encouraged to reach out and set me straight. As for everyone else … please enjoy the adventures of this Aramco Brat.

Richard P. Howard
Summer 2021

THE CRASH

Cairo, Egypt, Thursday, May 20, 1965, two a.m.

A Boeing 720B is in its second landing approach; the first attempt was aborted. The Cairo airport has just installed a new night-guidance landing system. Pakistan International Airlines (PIA) Flight 705 is inaugurating a new service: Karachi to London with intermediate stops in Dhahran, Saudi Arabia; Cairo; and Geneva, Switzerland. The plane is piloted and crewed by the airline's very best. There are 127 souls aboard, including twenty-two premier members of the Pakistani press who are likely to write about and thus promote the service. Ten Chinese Communists are passengers, including the chief designer of a jet fighter. (With a stop in Pakistan, this will be the fastest route between China and England.) A senior Egyptian diplomat and his wife are seated in first class. Also in first class, and one of four Americans aboard, is Donald D. Love, an Exxon executive specializing in aviation fuel. He is headed home via London to his daughter's wedding in Riverside, Connecticut, having recently left Hong Kong after a six-week assignment in East Asia. Arif Raza, whose father owns Hostellerie de France, a landmark Karachi airport hotel, is aboard. Mrs. F. N. Choudhury, pregnant, is flying to meet her husband in London. Travel agents, wooed for their potential to generate future agency business with complimentary tickets, fill out the manifest. The Kanoo Travel Agency of Al Khobar, Saudi Arabia, did not send a representative but at the last minute had assigned their three seats to the vacation travel itinerary of an American Aramco engineer and his family, who boarded in Dhahran and were headed to their son's high school graduation in Michigan. None were prepared.

Whether through pilot error (this was PIA's top pilot, and to his right was PIA's number two), mechanical problems (certainly possible), or the poor operation of the newly installed night-landing system (my guess), the 720B "touched down" in a level field about six miles south of the intended runway. It was nowhere near level enough. Moving at 150-plus miles an hour, the left wing hit first. It may have been tilted down at the moment of impact, or perhaps it encountered a small hillock, but in any event, it ripped off first. As the struts and housings holding the two massive Pratt & Whitney turbofan engines on that wing failed, the deadly innards sprayed in all directions. While the plane cartwheeled and slid haphazardly forward, both the nose and its right wing encountered obstacles. The pilots, and bridge area generally, were quickly crushed. The second wing snapped off and by then, with structural stresses far beyond the strength capability of the aluminum skin and internal framing, the middle of the plane ripped open. Passengers spilled out, some already dismembered. Eventually bodies and pieces of the shattered wreck came to rest over the space of about half a mile.

During the next few minutes, most of those not already dead succumbed to their wounds. Miraculously, about a dozen passengers remained alive. In the small first-class section forward, behind the crushed bridge, everyone was killed, but in a forward-aisle seat of tourist class there was a temporary survivor. Lewis P. Howard,

Map of Pakistan International Airlines (PIA) flight plan for their new Flight 705. It left Karachi on May 19, 1965. The final destination was London.

the Aramco engineer who'd boarded in Dhahran, was badly injured but alive. Next to him, his wife, Marian, and daughter, Elizabeth, were dead. The battering seems to have been particularly hard on smaller bodies—none of the twenty-three children and women aboard lived, including the four cabin attendants. One of whom, Momi Durrani, at that time the "face of PIA" in the airline's print advertisements, had been in the least-damaged rear of the plane. That is where Jalal-al-Karimi, a vigorous thirty-something-year-old, found that, other than being badly bruised, he was fine.

Despite the fuel burned during the 1,200-mile flight from Dhahran, there was certainly fire risk, and Howard, a U.S. Navy catapult officer in World War II, would have been keenly fearful. (Many victims were ultimately burned beyond recognition.) Regardless of who sounded the alarm, it was Karimi, the Dhahran-based PIA station manager, who acted. One by one he helped the survivors to a small nearby hillock. The miserable group looked out over the wreckage, mourning their friends, companions, and loved ones. Travel agent Shaukat A. Mecklai, whose wife was in a first-class seat, was alive and grieving. But by the very act of moving their battered bodies painfully to that hillock, they showed a determination to live. Perhaps they had other loved ones, perhaps they saw their life's work as unfinished, perhaps they were just ornery. In any case they were alive and most desperately needing medical help.

Would it come in time? They weren't that far from the airport. The control tower operators knew Flight 705 should have landed. They knew the radio connection had been broken. Surely help would come. Within minutes their hopes were raised only to be quickly dashed. First to the scene were not saviors but looters. Jewelry, particularly wedding and engagement rings, was a prime target. Where necessary, fingers of the dead were cut off. Somewhere in the wreckage a smallish shoebox full of diamonds headed to De Beers's London Central Selling Organization by confidential courier was found ... and kept. It must have been heartbreaking to watch.

As the minutes ticked slowly by, injuries and wounds winnowed the group. It took an unforgivable six hours for help to arrive, strengthening my conviction in the ground staff's incompetence and adding to my distrust of any information they later gave to accident investigators.* By then only Karimi, Mecklai, Raza, and three others were alive. Former Navy officer Howard was dead from his injuries, his wedding ring added to the loot and his remains later identified by his dental records. In total, 121 dead have their names memorialized on a stone monument in the Pakistani section of Cairo's Bassatine cemetery. Most are interred there, although Exxon flew Love's body home to his grieving family and a somber Connecticut wedding. None of the thirteen crew members survived. It was, at the time, the third worst single-plane disaster in aviation history. All Pakistan grieved. It changed my life ... I was Lewis Howard's eighteen-year-old son in Michigan.

---

* Accidents don't just happen; they are caused. Most often there are several contributing factors, and that is almost certainly possible in the case of Flight 705. Night landings are always more difficult and dangerous than daytime landings. Perhaps a balky

rudder or wind shear or other unknown factors all combined to cause the crash. More likely, though, the runway lights weren't on properly or the instrument landing system was improperly handled. What exactly happened and why will never be known. Not to be forgotten are the institutional pressures that influence any investigation. The airlines, airports, and plane manufacturers all seek to avoid financial responsibility. They typically shout "pilot error," pushing blame on the one actor whom it's not worth suing. Further, those three all have incentive to not point out the shortcomings of one another; their businesses are mutually dependent. In this case, according to the official investigation, the flight recorder supposedly indicated a shallow and then sharp descent until the aircraft hit the ground. It is hard to trust that information. Debris scattered over half a mile suggests a shallow descent. Other "facts" stated in the investigation, such as the time of the crash, are clearly wrong. Chapter 1 may not be perfectly accurate, but it is the best reconstruction possible. It draws upon virtually all available information about the crash. A Boeing investigation and numerous newspaper accounts, both at the time and subsequently, provided some key facts. Over the years, the date May 20 often brings forth new information in *Dawn*, Pakistan's premier English-language newspaper. Both Karimi and Mecklai have given many interviews recounting the crash. In addition, I have also considered privileged information, never made public, that surfaced with the litigation that followed the crash. Lastly, a conversation with De Beers in London confirmed the diamond shipment. Black boxes weren't introduced until 1967. Long before then, the Air Line Pilots Association, International (ALPA), citing poor lighting and runway operating conditions, had refused further night landings in Cairo. What more do you need to know?

NOMADIC YOUTH

Not quite 4,000 days before the Cairo crash, I could be found in Glenshaw, a suburb outside Pittsburgh, Pennsylvania. It was the day after Christmas, 1955. My father had joined giant Aramco (the Arabian American Oil Company) thirteen months before, and we would soon be with him in KSA, the Kingdom of Saudi Arabia. With Dad's employment (badge number 17208), I had become an Aramco Brat, a phrase with a parallel etymology to Army Brat. This identifier I initially found unfair but came to love. Now I was headed off to live the role. Before departure we'd been very busy—obtaining passports, selling our car, preparing our house for renters—added to what I imagine were Mom's many personal tasks. It had been a tough year for her, highlighted by three fender-benders, including one that had left me bloodied against a very unforgiving dashboard. Lucky for her, the policeman who witnessed the accident ordered her to leave the scene immediately and take me to the hospital ... we went home. Also painful for me were the shots and inoculations for all sorts of scary diseases, including smallpox, typhus, tetanus, and typhoid—about fifteen in all, spread out over four trips to the clinic.

A neighbor drove Mom, my almost-six-month-old sister Elizabeth (Beth), and a nine-year-old version of myself to the downtown Pittsburgh train station. It was my first time on a big intercity train, and we traveled stylishly in an old Pullman car through the drizzly day. After dark, Mom's older brother, Sam, a music professor at Juilliard, picked us up at Penn Station in New York City. He drove us to White Plains, where he and my aunt Alice had an apartment. My memory blurs concerning the next 30 or so hours but clears again for the late afternoon of December 28, with Sam driving us to Idlewild, which was later renamed John F. Kennedy International Airport.

We checked in for our flight on the *Oryx*, one of Aramco's three DC-6s. I was mildly disappointed not to

Within a few years of my arrival in Saudi Arabia, the only American on a drilling rig would be the foreman. Saudis had mastered much of this difficult and dangerous work.

be flying on the *Camel* or the *Gazelle*; I'd at least heard of those animals. What was an oryx? (Later I learned that, when viewed in profile and from just the right vantage point, this species of antelope appears to be a unicorn.) Boarding itself was fun: my responsibility the entire trip was to carry Mom's Irish harp (used in her professional folk-song concerts) while she carried Beth and associated baby paraphernalia. We also had a change of clothes in an Aramco carry-on bag and two big suitcases that were loaded into the baggage compartment. In those days there were no enclosed ramps leading to a plane's door; instead we struggled up slippery steps wheeled up to the plane. As a six-year-old, I had flown by myself from New York to Portland, Maine, but this was nothing like that commercial flight. The three of us were in the back of the plane in a small, semi-enclosed "first-class" section with one youngish couple. The husband left us when Mom nursed Beth to head up front and join a group of eight or so of the roughest-looking men I had ever seen. That group, a drilling rig crew, wasted no time in consuming alcohol in apparently unlimited quantities, all while being unfailingly friendly to me and courteous to Mom.* More jarring still was the jumble of equipment that filled the aisle and most of the

---

* In the mid 1950s only about six to ten wells were being drilled by Aramco each year. Today, about 200 rigs are running in KSA. For contrast, consider that about 10,000 wells have sometimes been drilled annually in North America. Also interesting: that rig crew I traveled with was soon obsolete. Within a few years Aramco rigs typically only had an American foreman, with the other crew members being Saudi nationals.

seats. Long pipes, chunky machinery, all kinds of priority items the oil company needed ASAP. It was enthralling.

The flight left on schedule. The flight attendant, a woman who must have had supreme self-confidence to deal with the fraternity up front, closed off our area and—presto—created four beds. Despite being incredibly excited, I soon fell asleep, the raucous voices mixing with the roar of the engines. We were headed east-northeast toward Gander, Newfoundland. When I awoke, it was pitch black outside the window and the plane had quieted except for engine noise. Hours passed, and eventually a smattering of lights appeared below—we were landing. It was my first night landing, and the first time I'd been in a foreign country.

Gander seemed much bigger than Idlewild, a huge airbase critical in World War II.* A little more than a decade earlier, thousands of bombers had landed there

---

* Gander was in fact the biggest airport in the world when it was finished in 1938. In 1955, flights crossing the Atlantic usually stopped there or in Ireland, or both, for refueling. With the introduction of larger planes in the 1970s, Gander steadily lost importance; it was maintained only because of its handy location in the event of emergencies. On September 11, 2001, as the United States closed its airspace in response to the terrorist attacks on the World Trade Center in New York City and the Pentagon in Washington, D.C., thirty-eight planes made emergency landings at Gander. The crews and passengers were marooned there for four days ... 7,000 extra people crammed into a town of 12,000. Their gracious reception was lauded by international media and later became the subject for the Broadway musical *Come From Away*. Very recently, my wife, Yvette, and I spent a day in New York City's theater district with the show's producer. This Aramco Brat has come a long way.

to refuel before heading to England and the fighting in Europe. Leaving the harp on the plane, the three of us walked to the terminal. The air was cool, damp, and windy, but not raining. Right away I noticed that none of the vegetation was more than eighteen inches high, and every green thing seemed to be permanently leaning with the wind. As Mom and Beth headed to the ladies' room for a diaper change and some nursing, one of the locals engaged me in some friendly conversation. "Where are you headed?" he asked. "Arabia," I responded. Out came an undecipherable Canadianism followed by, "What an adventure!" He sure had that right.

After the plane refueled, and we'd collected a much more subdued group of fellow passengers, we took off while it was still dark. I slept through the coming sunrise and much of the next fifteen or so hours. Did we land and refuel in Shannon, Ireland? Maybe. For sure we landed at Amsterdam's Schiphol airport in the afternoon. For the first time, we went through a foreign country's security, where there was some confusion when my sister didn't have her own passport (she was included in Mom's—whose dumb idea was that?). We were then driven to the Grand Hotel Krasnapolsky, where we spent the night. Believe me it *was* grand, as it would continue to be on our future one-night stops in Amsterdam (Aramco had a large office in the Netherlands and an ongoing relationship with the Krasnapolsky). Both drives to and from the hotel were seemingly in rush hour, and I saw masses of commuters on bicycles as well as the occasional bombed building, courtesy of the invasion by Germany during World War II. This was not Pittsburgh.

Mom, Beth, and I land at Amsterdam's Schiphol Airport. Aramco Brats of my vintage all seem to have a similar first trip to Arabia photo, although it might be snapped at Shannon, Ireland, or less likely Athens, Greece.

The next morning the *Oryx* took off again, continuing east. But somehow things were completely different. Now I was rested and an old hand, nothing was strange. Stepping over machinery, finding my seat, handling the harp, bantering with the roughnecks all came easily to me. Beth spent most of that day in my arms while Mom dozed as we flew on and on, stopping for fuel first in Rome and then in Beirut. I got off during both stops, determined to be able to say I had been "on the ground" in both Italy and Lebanon. None of my friends back home could say they'd been anywhere but Canada. I heard Arabic for the first time in Lebanon, and finally we headed for Dhahran, flying through the night.

• • •

Dawn, January 2, 1956, the sky a crystal-clear blue as the pilot announced ten-mile visibility. At first the ground we were flying over didn't look much like desert—at least it didn't look like the desert of French Foreign Legion films. Very little sand, mostly a gravelly plain. Mom jabbered constantly about getting off the plane, as excited as though she were about to play a concert. I tuned her out, thinking ahead to a hug from Dad as I handled the harp and my new responsibility, our carry-on bag. Mom would take infant Beth, who had endured the whole trip remarkably well, with very little crying—and when she did cry, it was always quietly.

Soon we were landing on a beautiful strip of black asphalt: Dhahran Airfield, Saudi Arabia. The weather was perfect, dry and cool. The terminal building was a half tube of rounded arching corrugated steel, a very large Quonset hut open at each end. *Confusion* seemed to be the operative word, with the Saudi officials trying to organize customs and general security, while the Americans kind of followed directions. Dad, a tall man, was easy to spot, but the group milling about kept us from getting close. Then Mom shouted "Lew!" in her booming operatic singing voice. He gave her a nod, which she obviously found inadequate, and eventually they made their way to each other and hugged. *This is really embarrassing,* I thought. Keeping the harp in a death grip as our flight's suitcases were dumped together on the ground, I watched as passengers sorted them out and moved on to customs, which involved opening the bags and, if nothing looked unusual, getting a chalk mark. I wouldn't let anyone touch, let alone chalk, the harp—and I kept thinking the whole time that if ever there were a way to bring in a tommy gun, this would be it.

It was late morning before we finally left the airfield in a taxi. The driver was from Somaliland, which I later learned was an African country where they spoke Arabic. Automobiles had only been recently introduced here, and in the mid 1950s, almost all taxi drivers in eastern Arabia were from Somaliland or Yemen/Aden. (I was surprised to learn that the first lesson of a truck-driver training course Dad had begun for Aramco workers was how to open the door. The second lesson? Don't get out until the vehicle has stopped moving.)

We headed toward Al Khobar. My view from the front seat was of sand in every direction. And this was sand that looked like it was supposed to—drifts ten feet and higher, with rippled patterns carved by the wind. The sand dunes rose slowly on the windward side and then dropped off sharply on the lee side. Almost always they were in the form of shallow crescents. The occasional metal sign, usually a Pepsi ad, was always pitted, the worse for wear. "Aren't there any Coke signs?" I asked my dad over the seat. "No, Coke has not respected the boycott." I wasn't exactly sure what a boycott was—but was certain I could respect it. "But we can drink Coke?" was my second question. "Nope, Coke is not allowed. But mostly you're not going to get that or other things because no one here wants them or can afford them." I'd spent the first six years of my life in three different miserable trailer parks and thought of myself as poor. So this place was really, really poor.

That impression strengthened as we entered Al Khobar, seemingly via the town's only paved street. The cross streets were all dirt. Our taxi was the only visible automobile among numerous rickety wooden carts pulled by donkeys. Some of the donkeys had red manes, which, Dad explained, meant their owners had made the pilgrimage to Mecca known as the hajj.

All the buildings were constructed of concrete, most only one story high, and everything was covered in dust and grime. We soon stopped in front of the three-story Al Suroor building and unloaded the taxi. Across the street an open lot smelled distinctly of urine, an impression confirmed the following morning.

Dad led us up one flight of stairs, then down a short hall to apartment *ithnayn*, number two. Inside were two bedrooms and a common room, with a kitchen nook holding a gas range/stove and a refrigerator. Since we would have electricity only for two to three hours each morning and two hours each evening, opening the refrigerator at other times was strictly forbidden. There would never be milk. Beth had a crib and I had a bed in the smaller of the two bedrooms. The common room had a card table, four metal folding chairs, and a plastic radio that Dad had bought. A strange wooden couch with cushions, a matching armchair, a small bookcase, and the beds were Aramco issue. Those were the furnishings … that's it. No telephone, no TV, but there was a balcony. That balcony figured in the very specific instructions I received that first night. Whenever I awoke and found my parents' door closed, I was to go out and notice everything unusual in the street scene. Over the next five months, that view and my activities on the ground below proved far more entertaining than television or movies. The trip was over; it was what I later thought of as my greatest trip—both an adventure itself and a start to ten years of further adventures. My nomadic youth as an Aramco Brat was launched.

"MAY GOD GIVE YOU STRENGTH"

Thanks to days of excitement and a completely discombobulated body clock, I went to bed early that first day in Al Khobar and slept soundly. I rose before the sun and, finding my parents' door closed, considered carefully my instructions from the night before. The lamp worked so the electricity was obviously on. Thirsty, I rejected (correctly, as it turned out) the water tap and opened the refrigerator. There wasn't much inside except a plastic pitcher filled with orange juice ... very refreshing ... and a quick look in the freezer section assured me there was more where that came from. It was full of frozen concentrated orange juice in cardboard tubes. Most of the staples in the cabinets didn't interest me, although I did find a box of grape Kool-Aid packets, which, in the days ahead, I would mix with the frozen juice concentrate and disgusting boiled or distilled drinking water that Dad brought, to create a brown but reasonably tasty drink concoction. (The tap water was suitable only for washing.) I also found some pretzels—past their prime but satisfying. The balcony beckoned.

The Suroor building roof and the balcony of our second-floor apartment were my favorite watching posts. The large building seen toward the Gulf also housed a number of Americans working for Aramco. None of the few other children were ever unsupervised on the street, to my knowledge. The minaret to the right of the picture was used for the call to prayer, five times per day. When it rang out, I was instructed to get home on the double. The religious police would come out with their sticks, sticks they often used.

The dawn twilight came and went quickly, and I watched the sun light up my new little town of about 5,000-plus as it came to life. There were a few automobiles—mostly taxis—on the street, but donkey carts predominated. The open lot across the street was, as I suspected the night before, the male urinal. As I watched, men wearing what appeared to be spotless white shirt-skirts would scrunch down, contort themselves a bit, and pee. They couldn't have been wearing underwear. A few pairs of men walked hand in hand—not something I'd seen before. It wasn't long before I heard the first call to prayer, melodic and rather pleasing. The men walking below quickened their pace, and suddenly there were about a half-dozen new men behind them, dressed similarly except for a thin, light tan over-jacket. Each carried what appeared to be an eighteen-inch-long hammer handle. Later that morning, Dad explained that these men were the religious police, and that on no account was I ever to have anything to do with them. The handles were not decorative. In fact, he said, whenever I heard the call to prayer, I was to get back to the apartment double-quick. Over the course of the next five months, I watched many threatening encounters and two beatings that amply convinced me of the soundness of this directive.

In 1956, January 3 was a Tuesday, and Dad explained that I'd be going to the Dhahran company school the following Saturday. *What?* Yes, Friday was the Islamic sabbath, Thursday there'd be no school, and that day Dad would work only until noon and be home early. His job was too far away—in Ras Tanura, with its big refinery and export terminal—for him to see us except on weekends and a usual Tuesday evening overnight. To this nine-year-old boy, it all seemed quite reasonable. Mom, however, was not really enamored with the situation. She responded by putting us to work cleaning the apartment with Brillo pads. Thank goodness for Beth. Whenever she needed changing or general comforting, I was quick to suspend cleaning and come to her aid. What had started as a day oozing excitement degenerated into drudgery.

The next day my life got better. In the morning, Dad and I took a taxi to Dhahran, Aramco's headquarters about ten or so miles from Khobar. As we drove around,

Dad pointed out the rec hall snack bar (where I'd be eating lunch) and, close by, the school. We got out and walked around that building; it was recess and kids who seemed to be to be perfectly normal were in evidence, with most looking like me. I could handle this. We picked up a few things at the company commissary, where Mom would be doing most of her shopping. Then the same taxi took us back to Khobar.

Later that day, I accompanied Dad to the money changers—a succession of small stalls, each maybe eight feet wide in front and eight to sixteen feet deep, containing one flinty-eyed entrepreneur, two customer chairs, a table, and bags of assorted change. Saudi Arabia had just recently introduced paper currency, but there were still slim wooden boxes designed to hold 1000 silver Riyals (each about the size of an American quarter) left over from the pre-bills era.* Less common, but still in use, were Maria Theresa thalers, a silver coin about the size and weight of a silver dollar. Paper U.S. dollars were well respected, and we got 3.75 Riyals for each. On the plane trip over, one of the roughnecks had given me a Dutch ten-guilder note as we departed Amsterdam. It was back in the apartment. Could I exchange it? Perhaps another day.

---

* Saudi paper money was introduced in 1952 or 1953, but it had a hard time gaining acceptance. The Ottoman Turk's sudden departure in 1915 from this area of Arabia had rendered much of their paper worthless, and the inhabitants had long memories. In 1956, the largest bill denomination was 20 Riyals, equivalent to $5.33 American.

Interspersed with the money changers were other shops, similar size or larger, most housed in one-story reinforced concrete buildings. They all had corrugated steel "garage door" fronts, the kind that you pulled down and secured with a padlock. That was the only way in or out. The shopkeepers and even the money changers were invariably friendly, perhaps not surprising as Americans had money and we were their best customers. Most offered us tea, which Dad said we should not accept unless we were sure we were buying something. He and the shopkeepers conversed in a sort of triple-threat language: English, Arabic, and gestures. I quickly learned how to say "How much?" and in a week or so learned the numbers one through ten, although the shopkeepers knew how to write them in English. One unusual shop caught my eye. It was a little bit bigger and more upscale than the others, with wooden display cases and, along with other items, model trains. Wow.

The main street had a sidewalk of sorts, otherwise we walked on hard-packed dirt. There was a pier that stretched into the Persian Gulf, mostly a rough jumble of stones. Soon Dad bought delicious, thin, just-baked bread, which we munched on. The bakery consisted of a large vertical hollow in a stone that had been well heated by a wood fire.

As we watched, the baker spread the dough on a wooden, tennis-racket-size spatula with a long handle. In a well-practiced motion, the baker reached the spatula in and slapped the thin dough against the inside wall of the stone. It stuck and cooked quickly, expanding into a bubble shape, and then the baker took it out of the oven

Buying bread was one of my favorite activities. It came out of this oven in a bubble shape, thin, crispy, and similar to naan. The cost was about two cents American. After leaving our Khobar apartment and moving into houses in the Aramco camps of Dhahran and the Ras Tanura, I often returned to the town on shopping and coin- or stamp-hunting trips. I always bought delicious just-baked bread.

with the spatula. In the future, I would be buying bread but only what I saw baked, never from inventory. Hygiene was not a Khobar strong point—hands were never washed, flies crawled over everything, and work surfaces were never cleaned.

My first full day out and about in Khobar was exciting but hardly idyllic. The animal and human smells were powerful, and I soon learned that they got a lot stronger when it rained. Most disturbing of all were the beggars. There were three distinct types: very occasional packs of four- to eight-year-old boys who focused on Westerners, single women (usually holding an infant and covered head to toe in black with only their eyes showing), and, less frequently, blind old men. Young boys, probably grandsons or nephews, led the latter home at mealtime. Flies constantly harassed us and them. I tried not to stare, but I watched in horror as flies crawled across the beggars' open eyes and the eyes of infants. Dad said that a horrible disease called trachoma, an eye infection that resulted in a crusty gunk on the surface and around the eyes, was spread by flies and could lead to blindness, which helped to explain the condition of the male beggars. (To this day I cannot stand a fly near my eyes.) Dad also gave me instructions on how to deal with the beggars: Never, never, never give them money. If you do it—even once—they will harass you every time you are on the street. Never be intimidated by the boys. Ignore old men and women. If you find yourself backed into a corner and desperate, say "May God give you strength" in Arabic. That phrase, plus "yes," "no," and "how much," were the day's language lesson.*

Looking back on that wonderful day sixty-five years ago, I have to wonder if Dad wasn't doing something that

---

* In the days ahead, I watched beggars and begging with great interest from my semi hidden balcony perch. It did not seem like a particularly remunerative activity. Saudi men never gave a coin to the women or boys, only to the old blind men. The women beggars seldom got handouts from anyone but other women, and there were few women on the street. These transactions were done very surreptitiously. The only time I saw the boy beggars get money was when they hounded an American woman so unmercifully that she threw a handful of change on the road before heading double-time to the Aramco bus. Dad was right about not giving money!

I didn't fully appreciate. He was a big, thirty-three-year-old man with naval officer command presence. Yes, he showed me the town and its many sights, but he was also showing *me* to the town. The Saudi people, particularly of that day, deserved their reputation of courtesy and kindness toward strangers and children. Regardless, the easy time I was to have there over the next five months may well have also stemmed from Dad's introduction.

DHAHRAN AND ITS SCHOOL

Saturday morning, January 7, 1956. Dad's carpool left at 6:00 a.m., headed toward Ras Tanura. I was picked up by taxi at 7:30 a.m. in front of the Al Suroor building. (By the way, *Al* in Arabic means "the," so it's dumb for me to keep saying "the" twice. I'll stop, even though no one has trouble with "the Los Angeles Angels," which in this context is dumb twice over.) Three girls were already aboard: a third-grade girl, who thought she was in charge, and two younger girls, one her sister. Occasionally we would pick up or drop off another elementary classmate who lived at the air base. Otherwise, it was a straight shot to Dhahran, through the security gate and to the school. Twenty minutes door-to-door, but two very different worlds centuries apart. I'm going to be in the fourth grade, despite the recommendation from my teacher in the States that this would be a good time to go back a grade.

Our taxi driver spoke English well and had been thoroughly vetted. Over the next months he was to prove both thick skinned (dealing with the third grader) and remarkably capable.* Every school-day morning our driver parked at the entrance to the girls' apartment building, about 100 yards from mine. One of the two mothers would shepherd in the girls and then they'd drive over to me. That first morning I was exemplary, later ... well, you know nine-year-old boys. To finish the topic: five minutes after the school day ended, we four would meet at a designated spot and taxi back to Khobar. Believe me when I say I never came close to missing that return ride; there was no plan B. The girls were dropped off first, but only after a mother came out to collect them. The few times that this didn't happen immediately, I would hop out and walk by myself.

---

* In May 1955, Dad's best safety inspector, a Palestinian, was summarily expelled from KSA. One morning he didn't show up for work and there were no goodbyes. He was suspected of agitating for a strike in Ras Tanura. The Saudi justice system was not incumbered by due process, particularly with regard to Palestinians. In June, just after we Howards moved out of Khobar, our taxi driver managed to avoid a nasty mob of Aramco's striking Saudi employees and deliver his passengers safely. There isn't much literature available concerning that strike. I do know what Dad told me: The strikers were shouting "death to the infidels," demanding more of what the Americans had (money, better living conditions, etc.), and blocking the main gate. None of this was conducive to Aramco productivity. In response, the government didn't adopt half measures; ten identified strikers were whipped until they revealed the names of the ringleaders, other strikers ... and probably, considering the pain, the names of everyone they knew. Once identified, other strikers and particularly the ringleaders were whipped until their accomplices and any outside agitators were revealed. Rinse and repeat. Needless to say, that was the last Aramco strike I was aware of during my time as a Brat.

A digression: Tim Barger, in his wonderful book *Christmas in Khobar*, talks about the day, circa 1956, when he went unescorted as a nine-year-old to Khobar. No doubt he did. But over the course of my five months as a Khobar kid, I never once saw any other unaccompanied American youth, although there probably were some. I was the only one consistently roaming the town. (At the risk of sounding judgmental, I think I can say Tim's Aramco Brat experience, as the son of a company president, was a bit different from mine. On the subject of the surprising and varied skills of Aramco workers, however, we are in complete agreement.) An older boy, Richard, who lived in our building, did play catch with me in the hall, and together we occasionally went up the two flights to the roof to watch the street scene below.

• • •

The Dhahran School itself was unremarkable, although the building was much nicer than the 1865 rat's nest that I had been attending in Pittsburgh. Our fourth-grade teacher seemed a competent woman who was used to the challenges facing new arrivals. She was, like all her fellow staff, a fully accredited American teacher. In fact, teleport Dhahran School into an upper-income American suburb and it would seem natural. I'll go one step further: teleport the whole city of Dhahran and—other than a dearth of the very rich, the poor, and the old—it would seem natural. My fellow students were not cliquish, and I soon had a friend. Terek Slim was the son of an attorney, a high-status position in a community composed mostly of middle-class and lower-middle-class white Americans with oil industry skills. At some point I got the impression that his family had fled Palestine when Israel was created. Neither I nor any other of my fellow students ever showed any sign of prejudice toward him or attributed any special status to the positions of our fathers.* I also remember a very nice girl named Penny, and another, whose name I've forgotten, who was determined to be better than me in math.

At 11:30 each morning, when class finished, I'd walk about five minutes to the snack bar, where I was to order a hamburger, fries, and Pepsi. Mom provided just the right funds. A few times over the next few months Terek joined me, but otherwise I was by myself as most everyone else went home for lunch. After eating, I was on my own as I didn't have to be back for the afternoon session until one p.m. What to do? It wasn't long before my meal became the snack bar's complimentary (soup) crackers and water. The money I saved I used to pay for two bowling games—the alley was next to the snack bar. My scores steadily improved, culminating in that wonderful game in which I rolled seven strikes, including five in a row. (Sixty-five years and many attempts later, that 177 score remains my best. Sad to peak at age nine.)

---

* From the vantage point of today, I have come to realize that for my parents, the general social scene in the Aramco camps was influenced by the work status of employees. Company towns are probably all alike in that regard.

In Pittsburgh, in a classroom of fifty-two pupils, I had learned that it was far better to "act up" when called upon than to appear ignorant in front of one's peers. The disruptions did not endear me to the teachers. Should I have been surprised when in first grade I was assigned to the "red" reading group? Well, I was surprised, and appalled to hear the names of its other members. In fact, other than winning the school's Chinese checkers tournament, being a standout at eraser tag (spit surreptitiously placed on the eraser before you put it on your head is a big edge), and being found to need glasses despite trying to memorize the eye chart, nothing much good happened to me in Pittsburgh.

Bottom line: Here I was in the fourth grade, and while I recognized a lot of words, I couldn't spell them and basically couldn't read. Dhahran School, however, with its much smaller, thirty-three-pupil class size, was not the place for acting up. Did I study hard? No, but I did stay at the top of the math group and gradually improved otherwise. I owe the Aramco schools a lot.

Come early May 1956, Dhahran and Khobar began sprucing up. King Saud was coming for a visit. During the last royal visit a few years before, everyone who had put up a triumphal arch on or along the king's path received a handsome monetary reward. This had not gone unnoticed, and nobody was going to miss out on such a potential windfall—arches sprouted up everywhere. When the day arrived, a line of black Cadillacs entered Dhahran and parked near the dining hall. I was on Dad's shoulders near the front of Aramco well-wishers, about twenty feet from the red carpet. First to get out of the cars was a black slave raised with the royal family who served as a personal bodyguard. Next was the king, whose father Abdelaziz—commonly called Ibn Saud—had reestablished the kingdom. Behind him, an entourage of princes and important folk streamed out. History has judged Saud harshly, and I wouldn't disagree, but at that place and time he sure looked impressive to me. Only one in the party wore the Arabian standard *gutra,* a red-and-white-checked head covering. Dad whispered that he was Ibn Jiluwi, governor of the Eastern Province, where we were. The guy looked about a hundred years old and as if he'd been in as many

I was on Dad's shoulders about 20 feet from the king and his entourage when they visited Dhahran in May 1956. The king sure looked impressive to me, although it was Ibn Jiluwi, the governor of the Eastern Province, who gave me an always-to-be-remembered look when Dad whispered his name. In this photograph that ran in the newspaper Sun and Flare, *he has on a red-and-white-checked* gutra *(headdress) and is to the king's left.*

knife fights. His hearing, however, must have been pretty good; Dad's whisper generated a hard look. I learned later that Jiluwi's father was Saud's father's first cousin. The two of them had captured Riyadh in fierce hand-to-hand fighting back in 1902. Apparently, the governorship was henceforth a hereditary position. Father and then son had held it since Hofuf, the capital of the Eastern Province, was captured from the Ottomans around 1915.

KHOBAR KID

During that first week, I found that there was often an enthusiastic game of soccer going on right inside Al Suroor when I got home. The ground floor of this newly constructed building had been designed with the idea that typical shops would be completed along the front, and possibly along the back, of the structure. In between was a space about 10 feet wide and 120 feet long, open at both ends. Other than the minor opening of the central stairway, it was perfect for a sort of indoor, off-the-wall, and off-the-ceiling soccer. The boys playing were about my age, and at one point they needed a player to balance sides. Starved for physical activity, I joined, quickly demonstrating an incredible lack of skill. No problem—every team needs a goalie … I never played any other position. Were there language problems? Not really. "Yes" and "no" combined with "go" and a strange word *yallah*, which pretty much meant move with vigor—those were all that were needed.

Another of my activities that did not start auspiciously but had terrific long-term benefits began by realizing that my Dutch ten-guilder note needed changing. I walked to Dad's money changer and with a smile and gesture asked for a transaction. In return, I received a smile, a headshake, and a display of coins and bills that I might want to buy. It had all looked so easy when Dad did it. After failing with another money changer, I returned home quite discouraged. That weekend Dad took matters into his own hands and failed just as I had—three times. "Not to worry," he said. The next weekend we would go to some real banks as soon as he got home, and we did. First up was the British Bank of the Middle East (I think Hong Kong and Shanghai Bank took it over a few years later). No luck. Next, we went to the only other bank, a Dutch bank. Again, no luck changing Dutch money at a *Dutch bank!* The manager, who must have realized my disappointment and perhaps felt a little guilty, invited us into his office and plied us with tea and conversation. There I heard for the first time about exchange rates, oil production, and banking. My bill was too small to be worth anything in Khobar, but the experience gained from trying to change it was priceless.

Al Suroor had, if I remember correctly, sixteen small apartments, eight each on the second and third floors. Aramco employees, tired of waiting for family housing in Dhahran, accounted for more than half the residents. It was a motley group, mostly Americans. Victor Vella and his wife, who lived next door, were from Malta. Mr. Vella worked in Aramco's Dhahran computer center and was home every night. He was crazy about photography and eager to explain its many nuances to anyone who would listen, including me. (Thanks to him,

I pushed Beth on her stroller throughout my little town of Khobar. We both were happy to escape the small apartment and Mom's singing. The rough jumble of stones behind her was the pier, where much of Aramco's small early equipment was landed. When the Ras Tanura refinery was constructed, heavy loads were dragged on the beach near our eventual home. Later when the marine terminal was completed, general cargo was unloaded at one of four docks. Oil tankers picking up cargos used the others. About the time of our arrival in Saudi Arabia, the new port of Dammam was handling almost all general cargo.

Dad bought a quality camera and took many of this memoir's photographs.) He also regaled me with stories of Malta's suffering during World War II. (The Vellas would later leave their wonderful cat with us when they departed Saudi Arabia two years later.) The women would shop in pairs, share cooking ingredients, and take the Aramco bus to and from Dhahran together. Looking back, I realize how different all the residents were, but with everyone under similar pressures, they consistently supported and helped each other. These were adaptive people.

Gradually, over the weeks of early 1956, I assumed more family responsibilities beyond taking care of Beth, although I still relished my time with her. (Her first step was into my arms, and when it came, her first word was *brother*.) I was sent to buy minor items at the shops, exchange small amounts of money, and take my sister for rides in a small stroller we acquired.

Beth would squeal with delight when we raced full speed along the few sidewalks. What must the locals have thought? At one point I noticed an envelope on a money changer's table with interesting postage stamps. They were British, featuring King George VI, but from Aden with local Adenese scenes. Seeing my interest, the owner carefully ripped off the corner of the envelope and gave it to me. Thereafter I started asking for stamps whenever I went to a shop and was often rewarded. Shopkeepers, and money changers in particular, seemed to get letters from faraway places. I began a haphazard stamp collection: Aden, Malta, Cyprus, Pakistan, Lebanon, and India, predominantly. Eventually I got an album and focused on stamps of countries that featured pictures of Queen Elizabeth or George VI.*

By being always around, I had become largely invisible to the shopkeepers and their customers. I didn't just buy things myself. I watched and learned while other people bought things. Americans, particularly American couples, were much too impatient. They would decide on something they wanted to buy and then hurry to close the transaction. Single American men might devote a little more time and usually at least tried to bargain, particularly if the item cost more than a few dollars. Saudi men were the masters. They acted like they had all day, always starting with traditional greetings and never really giving any early indication of which item they were interested in buying. I practiced the Saudi approach with my family's purchases and steadily improved. By midyear we Howards had developed solid shopping tactics. My parents would

---

* Ten years later, I sought to test out of a required college world civilization class so that I could take an extra engineering one. The rather grumpy professor verbally asked me a few questions, which I successfully answered, and then handed me a list of more than 100 countries. "Correctly pick out twenty that are in the British Commonwealth of Nations, and I'll sign off on this," he said. About a minute later I had an even grumpier professor and four college credits. Stamp collecting had paid off. It paid off again when I was interviewing for my first investment position. The CIGNA human resources professional asked if I'd done any collecting as a child and was pleased that I had. His thinking was that a young mind that organized information and stamps was a mind that was naturally inclined to organizing financial information. Sigh ... if it were only so easy.

cruise the shops, pick out what they wanted, price it, and be sure to price a few other items, while I watched. Then we would all leave. Later, I would return and begin haggling. I almost never offered a lower price; I just said the shopkeeper had to lower his … and he usually did. Of course, part of my success can be attributed to the fact that shopkeepers needed the transactions more than

My youthful postage stamp collecting began when a shopkeeper, seeing my interest, ripped off the corner of a letter and gave me these stamps. Aden at the time, thanks to its strategic location and fine harbor, was the second-busiest port in the world and had been under British rule for more than a hundred years. Locals had mastered the modern skills needed there, including ship repair and refueling (this explains their presence in eastern KSA as drivers). Similar stamps from British Commonwealth nations, with pictures of Queen Elizabeth II or her father, George VI, and featuring local scenes, were gradually added to my collection.

I did. My biggest triumph was buying a large beautiful Persian brass tray for $50 when my parents were prepared to pay twice as much and the asking price was higher still.

While chronologically not strictly accurate, Dad and I had another great Khobar-type adventure later in 1956. Five years before, a 350-mile railroad had been completed from the new port of Dammam to Riyadh, Saudi Arabia's capital. (In those days, Dammam was about ten miles from both Khobar and Dhahran. Today, all three have grown into one five-million-person metropolis.) Previously, a centuries-old caravan route had been the only land access into the center of the country. Now the railroad was taking more and more of the freight traffic between Riyadh and the coast. Dad was afraid shipping by camel was doomed and wanted to see the caravans before they disappeared. So we signed up for an extracurricular employee trip of about a hundred miles to Hofuf, one of the largest oases in the world. It was a traditional transshipment point, where caravans from Qatif on the Gulf coast, near Ras Tanura, would meet caravans from Riyadh and swap cargos. We traveled pleasantly on the railroad in an air-conditioned, self-propelled Budd Car with a group of other Aramco employees and families. Hofuf did not disappoint. The Budd Car let us out near the market square by the old fort, with its walls made of stone, adobe, and mud, which hadn't yet deteriorated with time and neglect. The active market featured goods from all over the world. Camels walked round and round pumping water from the sweet-water wells. Most exciting for Dad was that we were there when a caravan came in. It was only three camels, not the number we were hoping to see, but something.

A newly completed railroad was certain to drive the long-distance camel caravans out of existence. Dad took this picture on our trip to Hofuf, one of the largest oases in the world. He was disappointed it was only three camels ... a world thousands of years old was ending.

The old ways were ending in many ways. On the waters of the Gulf and on the beach near Khobar, you'd still see the occasional dhow, the classic Arab sailing ship built of teak and made to last. At that point in time, most of the ships were thirty years old or more, although some new ones were being constructed. Most had been built for the pearling industry (there were piles of discarded oyster shells on the beach), which began dying around 1930 when the stock market crashed, driving down the price of pearls by 90 percent. The industry then suffered a second, longer-lasting blow when the Japanese perfected cultured pearls. I believe that some modest amount of pearling was going on when I first went to Arabia, but I never saw it.

Near the end of my time living in Khobar, there occurred an experience that I carefully never shared with my parents but amply justifies my love of the Saudi people. The days had become a bit longer and I was out late visiting my favorite shop, the one with wooden display cabinets. The model train (H-O, for you aficionados) was hooked up and, just for me, was puffing around a small figure-eight track. I wanted to know everything about it. Just then the call to prayer ran out. I ignored it and kept asking questions. The shopkeeper got a worried look on his face, but I was a frequent customer and he want to sell the white elephant that had probably been in his shop for at least six months. As the minutes passed, he got more and more worried. Finally, I got worried. It was too late to get home. The religious police, with their sticks, were out in force urging the tardy to the mosques and banging on the shutters of any shops still open. What to do? My hero pulled down his steel shutter but left it about eighteen inches from closing. He could have closed it all the way, but that might have scared me and would hardly have looked proper. I was motioned to sit in a chair at the far back corner of the shop while he sat in the other back corner. His risk was even greater than mine, and terror showed on his face. Slowly the minutes ticked by. Happily, the police must have found someone else to absorb their righteousness, as they never came. I scrambled home as soon as prayer finished with a memory I will carry to the grave.

In 1956, Ramadan, the lunar month of daytime fasting for Muslims, began about the middle of April.

During Ramadan, the devout neither eat nor drink during daylight hours. I'm sure, as is the case of all religions, there were Muslims who didn't live up to this canon, but I only saw compliance in Khobar. As for me, Dad was very specific: "You will not eat or drink when outside our home." No ambiguity in that statement. But how about when I'm at school in Dhahran? He softened, reminded me to be respectful, and allowed that my lunches were okay. He didn't know it, but my lunches were pretty close to fasting already.

Two other aspects of that and my future Ramadans deserve mention. First, when did daylight officially end? Simple, stand where there is no moonlight and hold both a white and black thread at arm's length. When you can no longer differentiate, have a quick drink and serve up dinner. I'm sure today there is a more scientific method, but this worked fine back in the day. Second, since the Muslim year is based upon twelve cycles of the moon, it is about a dozen days shorter than a Western year. This made perfect sense in the medieval Arabian desert—how better to keep track of passing days and years? But as such, Ramadan slowly moves through the seasons. It was no problem in April 1956, but how about twenty years in the future? Then it's going to be falling in the brutally hot summer months. How was Aramco going to function? Well, my Bratdom ended long before that problem surfaced.

In May, Aramco made my mother very happy—we would soon be moving into the home of a Dhahran employee who was visiting the States on an eighty- to-ninety-day leave. Later, if our own house currently under construction in Ras Tanura was not finished, we would move into another temporary home. As it happened, we did use two Dhahran homes in this way, making our final move around September 1, in time for me to start the school year in Ras Tanura. I had not formed close attachments with any of the Saudi boys I played soccer with and soon forgot them. The shopkeepers and money changers were another matter. In the years that followed, we would continue our family shopping tactics when in Khobar, but of course there was much less occasion to do so since we were farther away and had easy access to Aramco commissaries. Six years later, however, my easy comfort with them was to pay unexpected dividends.

CRUSADER CASTLES

It was spring 1956 when Dad began talking about Crusader castles. In late 1954, he had spent three weeks in Sidon, Lebanon, for an Arabic language orientation. There he met William Eddy, the translator for the famous meeting of King ibn Saud and President Roosevelt near the end of World War II. (Thomas Lippman, in his 2008 biography of Eddy, also identifies him as head of the CIA in the Middle East.) Dad must have liked Eddy, or at least his sense of humor, as he kept an autographed copy of his book, *50 and one Jests of Goha*. In his free time Dad visited the picturesque castle situated at Sidon's port. He also traveled high above the Litani River to see nearby Beaufort Castle, which was rather derelict. Now he was due for a two-week vacation, and he wanted to tour Krak des Chevaliers in Syria. Krak was considered by T. E. Lawrence (aka Lawrence of Arabia, who in World War I blew up numerous Ottoman trains throughout present-day Arabia, Jordan, and Syria) to be the finest castle ever built. We would leave Beth with friends in Dhahran and fly to Beirut. Mom and Dad would enjoy the Saint George Hotel beach, and then after two days we'd rent a car and driver. (On future stops,

Mom and Dad always stayed at Le Commodore Hotel.) The driver, named Abraham, already knew my father well, and the two of them held discussions long into the night concerning how to set up a taxicab operation. The company was to be called Radio Taxi (as every vehicle would have a radio), and within a few years it was in existence. Last I knew, the company was still going, although without radios.

Abraham knew every road in Lebanon. We started by visiting Byblos Castle, north of Beirut. Although the Mediterranean view was fine, there was nothing fairy tale about it. A square layout, with towers on each corner, Byblos was utilitarian from top to bottom. Interestingly, Abraham pointed out the fascinating use of old Roman marble columns. Consider an outer wall whose base was 20 feet thick. On the outside skin were consistent, very closely fitting stones measuring 24 by 36 inches and 24 inches thick. No mortar joints. On the inside: much less consistency and mortar joints. Between these two skins the Crusaders dumped broken rock (there must have been plenty) and filled in any voids with mortar. The resulting wall performed very satisfactorily against attackers but was vulnerable to earthquakes. The solution, when available, was to put old 20-foot columns crosswise between the two skins. The twelfth-century equivalent of rebar.

Krak des Chevaliers, on the other hand, looked spectacular. Two concentric walls, the inner one 100 feet high and 80 feet thick at its most vulnerable point. The outer wall was 40 feet high and made to seem higher by the surrounding dry moat. After visiting modest Byblos, this was stunning. Krak was situated about twenty-five miles

CRUSADER CASTLES 47

LEBANON Vacation - 1956
The country is about 120 miles long by 40 miles wide

Other than the occasional weekend hour in early 1956, this Lebanon trip was my first time with Dad in 18 months. We talked about fortifications, the advantages and disadvantages of square versus rounded tower shapes, and the place in history of the Phoenicians and Crusaders. We talked and talked. The pass at Dog River was of particular interest to Dad. Armies moving either north or south had to move though this choke point or otherwise go far inland. In 1918 General Allenby's British army had gone through, leaving a carved memento celebrating their accomplishment. Many others, including Alexander the Great and his army, did the same.

inland, high on a mountain spur overlooking a beautiful valley. Abraham timed our drive to arrive as dawn broke, so that we looked through the darkness around us and saw the castle far above, outlined by the sun. We were the only visitors that morning and had the run of the place. I had a great time, sitting where the senior knights had their evening meal, drinking water from a still-functioning cistern, and surveying both the innards of the fortress and the valley scene from the commandant's office. Climbing the circular stone steps to this office, I noticed a distinct reduction of wear the higher the floor, until at the top everything looked brand new. Also interesting was how, before climbing the last two flights of stairs, you had to cross a tower room where the junior knights slept, which added a formidable challenge to possible nighttime assassins. I was ready to sign on as commandant.

The magnificent Crusader castle, Krak des Chevaliers, just over the Lebanon border in Syria.

Krak is a UNESCO World Heritage site, so any further description is unnecessary here. But Abraham did point out something not likely found in today's tourist brochures. Among the packs of ragged, shoeless children in the small village below the castle were a significant number of blonds. He would shout "Crusader!" at every sighting, confident that the long-ago mixing in of Frankish DNA, and with it the blond hair of northern Europeans, had not been completely diluted by the passing of 700 years.

Among other locations we visited on that trip were the castle at Tripoli, the pass at Dog River, and the Baalbek Roman ruins, another spectacular UNESCO World Heritage site. Dog River, in particular, captured Dad's attention. Abraham explained that here the mountains crowded the sea and each other. An army moving either north or south along Lebanon's coast either went through

Mom and I watch as Abraham, our driver, draws water from the 800-year-old cistern of Krak des Chevaliers.

the small Dog River pass or needed to go far inland. It was pretty clear that armies had gone through the pass, many recording their accomplishment on the rock walls. I remember seeing the Greek one carved by Alexander the Great's army. There were plenty in Arabic writing, and only one in English, General Sir Edmund Allenby's of 1918.*

I look back with nostalgia on that 1956 Lebanon trip. Other than the occasional day in Khobar, this was the first extended time I'd spent with Dad in eighteen months. We talked about the advantages and disadvantages of square and round towers in fortifications. We talked about Phoenicians and Crusaders and their place in Lebanon's history. We talked and talked. The trip sparked a lifelong interest in the Crusades and contributed to my own family visiting the castles of Wales twenty-five years later.

---

* Twenty-five months after our visit, President Eisenhower ordered the landing in Lebanon of a 5,000-man Marine contingent to "protect the legitimate government," a phrase that has lost a good deal of its validity in the years since. In case you're wondering, they came nowhere near the Dog River pass. For the past fifty years I have believed they landed on the Saint George Hotel beach. From there they quickly advanced to the airport while passing by the school I was to attend three years later. It was an operation planned with Normandy in mind, but instead of Nazis, the Marines were met by enterprising youths selling soft drinks and by bikini-clad beauties (few if any seeking suntans). Well, in fact-checking for this memoir, I found that a few days before the landing, the Marines sent an officer in civilian garb to provide an updated reconnoiter of the Saint George Hotel beach—and he chose one of the hotel's similar secondary beaches a few miles away. In other respects, my memories are reasonably accurate.

THE DHAHRAN-RT ROAD

As the crow flies, it's about twenty-five miles between Dhahran and Ras Tanura, or RT. Not that there were many crows or birds of any kind in 1956 eastern Arabia. The road in those days was perhaps twice that distance, however. Part of the reason was RT's location on its peninsula, but a much bigger factor was the existence of what is known as sabkha, a mixture of sand and semi-evaporated sea water in large "bays" along the shore. It appears to be solid, particularly at low tide, and usually has a blue-white tinge to its sandy appearance. At high tide, however, it is very definitely *not* solid—as water from Tarut Bay gradually seeps in, it leaves an unsupported crust. It must have been low tide on my first drive to Ras Tanura, because there were two Saudis out using their hands to scrape up and bag the salty residue from the crust's top. Dad again had specific instructions for me: "Stay off the sabkha—it can be quicksand." And: "If you find yourself in quicksand, get horizontal immediately and swim out of the muck."

A dozen-plus years in the future, King Faisal would create an independent, all-powerful agency to manage

The road from the Dhahran area to Ras Tanura was much longer than you would think, as it moved well inland to get around the sabkha (a mixture of sand and semi-evaporated seawater). When conditions were just right, a thin layer of nearly pure sea salt would accumulate, which these two Saudis are harvesting by hand. More likely, conditions would result in quicksand—salt was unusual, quicksand was common.

the modernization of Jubail, a small fishing village north of Ras Tanura. Jubail had a similar sabkha problem. After much study (there's always an overpaid consultant), the obvious solution was adopted and the area was crossed with several drainage canals and then huge quantities of sand were used to raise the land's elevation by six feet. In 1956, Aramco wasn't prepared to spend that kind of money, and so the road looped around the sabkha much farther than otherwise appeared necessary.*

At about the road's halfway point, near the Qatif Oasis, there was a small, dilapidated one-story building. This was supposedly a customs collection point, a reminder that Qatif, and Traut Island just offshore, were once key gateways into central Arabia. It was through these ports that processed dates were exported, as the Riyadh, Hofuf, and Qatif oases produced far more dates than were consumed locally. They had been Arabia's most important cash crop for centuries. In return, all manner of imports flowed in, with teak logs used in roof construction being a particular need in the times before reinforced concrete. Dates, along with the spending of Muslim pilgrims visiting the holy cities of Mecca and Medina on the annual hajj, were pretty much all of KSA's revenues in those pre-oil days. This was a poor place.

But it hadn't always been poor, as indicated by the presence of two derelict stone towers farther on toward Ras Tanura. They were each about a half mile in shore from the road and about three miles apart, parallel to the road. While we only noted them on that first drive, we thoroughly explored them in the days ahead. Climb in

---

* On a Boy Scout trip a few years later, we flew over Jubail. Its most fascinating feature was several semicircular rock rubble walls, ends anchored at the shore that extended into the Gulf. At high tide, unsuspecting fish would come in and be trapped when the tide went out, making for an easy catch. I mention this because nowhere else in the Aramco area did I see evidence of this economic activity.

and you could see water below. Climb down about five feet below the surface of the surrounding land and you could see a tunnel entering at twelve o'clock and exiting at six o'clock below the water's surface. The towers were part of a long-abandoned irrigation system built to keep sand from blowing into these inspection and maintenance points. After studying it, Dad was convinced that the tunnel extended about 300 miles, and that it brought water all the way along the western shore of the Gulf, from the Tigris-Euphrates river system to Qatif and perhaps beyond. (Hopefully someday, someone with credibility will reach a similar, more "official" conclusion.) At one point, after a trip to Iran, Dad came home having discussed the RT tunnel and its technology with artisans and scholars responsible for studying and maintaining similar medieval systems. I remember one specific factoid: To maintain grade in those pre-laser days, a waxed string about six feet long was stretched taut. A small drop of water was placed at the midpoint. If it stayed there the end points were level with one another. Genius.

Exactly when the system was built and how long it operated aren't known. But it is easy to guess why it fell into disuse. Such a system needs a strong central government. Locals concerned with their own economics wouldn't necessarily be focused on water users down the line. For 400 years the Islamic empire—ruled first from Mecca, then Damascus and later Bagdad—was the world's most enlightened political entity, and it's reasonable to assume that it was during that period that the irrigation system was developed and eastern Arabia thrived. After the Mongol's horrific 1258 sack of Bagdad,

On the road to Ras Tanura there was both old and new. In the picture above I'm examining the inside of a derelict tower that kept sand from blowing into an old irrigation system. Dad believed that the system brought water from the Tigris-Euphrates river system all along the western side of the Arabian Gulf to the Qatif Oasis and perhaps beyond. Hopefully a scholarly study will verify his supposition.

however, it was just a matter of time before this complex began its inevitable decline.

My first view of the Ras Tanura refinery. Note how Dad, the budding photographer, was always trying to get camels into his pictures to stress the old and new. Today I'm struck by how very modest the refinery looks. The past 65 years have seen enormous additions of equipment and plant designed to wring the most out of the crude oil processed. The smoke in the picture is a thing of the past. Today Aramco captures almost all of the natural gas produced in association with the crude and uses it to power its own operations and the economy of Saudi Arabia.

BOILING POINT

Ras Tanura, unlike almost all other Aramco locations, has been "on the map" (or, more accurately, British maps) for perhaps 200 years. It was chosen, quite sensibly, to be the site of Aramco's shipping terminal and refinery as the only logical place near the early oil discoveries where deep water nears the shore. From here, a narrow spit of land about seven miles long heads in a southeasterly direction into the Gulf, with the piers of the terminal near the very end. If you walk or drive those miles, the Gulf is on your left, while on your right is Tarut Bay. Just beyond the horizon to the right is Tarut Island, with its sixteenth-century Portuguese fort. Together, that island and the Ras Tanura peninsula crimp the opening of the bay. At high tide, the shallow bay, which I'd guess is about 100 square miles, fills with water. As the tide turns and falls, a huge amount of water now has to flow out of the bay and back into the Gulf through a relatively small opening. Particularly near the tip of the spit a rip tide, dangerous to swimmers with its swirling, bubbling water, occurs. After ebb tide, water begins rushing back into the bay with the same result, different direction.

Locations in Arabia are typically named for the resident tribe or after a distinguishing physical feature. Khobar, for example, was named for the local tribe. Dhahran was named for the symmetrical *jebel,* or large hill, nearby (which I would eventually climb with an old driller who had spent years in Nicaragua and regaled me with his stories. But back to Arab place-names). Abqaiq, another Aramco town in the Eastern Province, I've been told, can be translated as "land of many flies," but let's be charitable and reject that translation. This brings us to Ras Tanura. Before Aramco arrived, this area was uninhabited, with Qatif and Tarut both being a good fifteen miles away. It's in my amateur linguistic opinion that the word *tanura* derives from a very hot stove with bubbling steamy water. I'm on firmer ground with *ras,* Arabic for a point or head of land jutting into the sea. Avoiding and ignoring conflicting facts, I've concluded that Ras Tanura should be translated as "boiling point." As one of the most critical locations for the successful operation of the world's economy, it deserves a dramatic name. In any event, this is where our family went to live in early September 1956. Dad had been working here as a district safety engineer since January 1955, residing in a bunkhouse with three other men. It was obvious to me that he loved our new hometown and having his family with him. Left behind were Khobar and Dhahran, but we could and would enjoy visits to both in the years ahead.

That first visit, while waiting at the security gate to enter the compound, a mile or two north of the spit's base, Dad's boosterism began. "See that stoplight? It's the fourth stoplight installed in the whole kingdom." We hadn't gone

MY WORLD within RAS TANURA

My Daily World in the NAJMAH

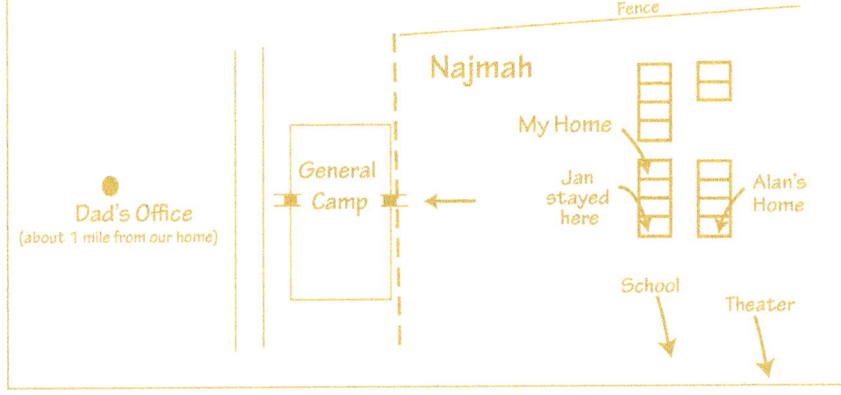

In September 1957 we moved to Ras Tanura … my literal translation: Boiling Point. This is one of the most important places in the world's economy; it deserves a dramatic name.

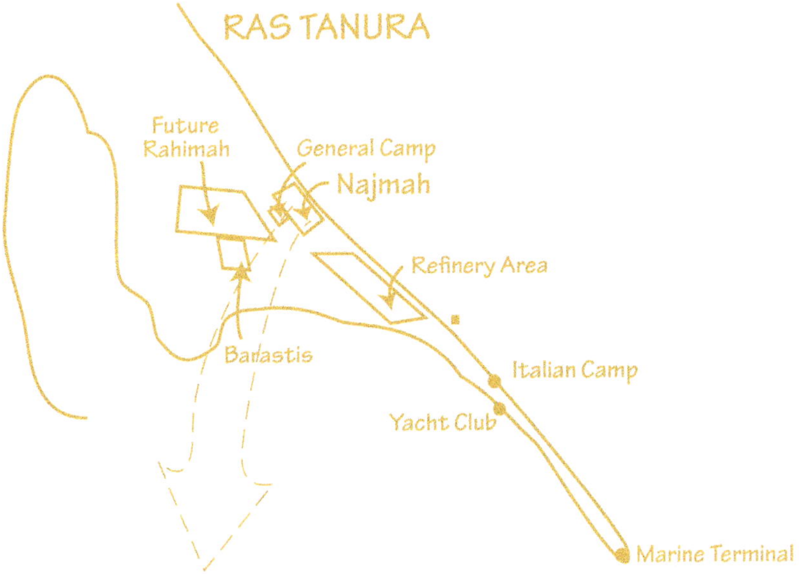

fifty feet when he piped in again: "See that stoplight at the refinery entrance? It's Saudi Arabia's first stoplight." More stories followed of Florence Chadwick, the first woman to swim the English Channel in both directions, training for her ocean swim right off our beach. It all added to the glamour of Ras Tanura. I was most intrigued with the physical presence of several solid stone buildings. It seems that during World War II, a large group of Italian soldiers stationed in Eritrea, on the other side of the Red Sea from Arabia, had surrendered to the British Army and become prisoners of war. As the war was ending, these POWs with masonry skills were offered a choice: go home to unemployment in a war-ravaged Italy or work for Aramco. Quite a few chose the second option, living in their own camp about halfway between the refinery and the terminal. That camp's most interesting relic was a patio floor of upside-down wine and liquor bottles filled with sand. Arabia was officially "dry" during my time as a Brat, but it sure hadn't been for the Italians.

At this point, even as a child, I realized that our town had some very different parts, although throughout my time there, Ras Tanura was the only name I used. The refinery and terminal were separate entities. A third area, Najmah, was about two miles north of the main security gate, with that distance a safety feature. Najmah possessed a beautiful beach, a stone theater, the stone surf club, and our brand-new home: a three-bedroom, 1,200-square-foot row house. This was where all Americans and Western Europeans lived, even those without senior staff pay grades. Outside the main security gate was a golf course of sorts, with "greens" of oiled sand and specific rules I never bothered learning—trailer park boys don't play golf. We also had easy access to the now abandoned Italian camp and a small "yacht club" dock near that camp in Tarut Bay.*

A fourth part of RT was the general camp, made up of very spartan multi-occupancy male dorms for Indians, Pakistanis, Palestinians, and assorted other non-senior-staff foreigners. The camp was adjacent to Najmah's west side and could be accessed through a pedestrian security gate. Even though all of these areas had various levels of individual security and fencing, I mastered moving between them unhindered within a few months. Outside these very orderly Aramco-controlled entities there was squalor. Grubby Khobar was nirvana in comparison.

Most of Aramco's Saudi employees and their families lived in a fifth part of Ras Tanura, a ramshackle collection of one- and two-room shacks called *barastis* that had ceilings only about four feet high. The roofs were made from the flattened sides of 55-gallon oil drums, the walls

---

* The rip tide and the refinery were not Ras Tanura's only dangers. A few months after we moved in, while wading at the yacht club beach, little two-year-old Beth was stung by a Portuguese man o' war. The jellyfish, which I had barely noticed and mistaken for an innocent weed, nearly paralyzed her, wrapping its tentacles around her upper arm. Luckily, I was nearby and scooped her screaming body up out of the water. We rushed her to the health center. More common and much less dangerous jellyfish often stung me during my RT years. I was far more wary, however, of the occasional deadly sea snake. Accepted wisdom was that their mouths were too small to endanger humans. I was not convinced and immediately exited the water the few times I saw one.

In 1956 almost all of Aramco's Saudi employees working in Ras Tanura lived in this shanty town. The shacks, known as barastis, *had roofs of flattened oil drums and walls woven from palm fronds. The decrepit trailer parks of my early years looked positively welcoming in comparison.*

of woven palm fronds reinforced at the corners with discarded packing crate boards. The better huts might have had carpet floors, but many did not. There was no sewage system and there were few if any communal water taps. It was a rabbit warren of twisted pathways, none more than four feet wide, as friends and relations tried to share common walls for companionship, warmth, and security. My first look convinced me not to go there, and I never did again. Little did Dad or I know that a year later this squalor would represent his great challenge and opportunity.

Just as I was starting fifth grade, there occurred one of those little "pebble in the pond," "butterfly flapping its wings" events that ripple into something truly important.

Fishing off the terminal's pier at dawn (I'm the first figure in the right foreground). The sun, just coming up to the east, silhouettes a tanker loading. Notice the rows of pipe behind me. Besides crude oil the terminal exported the refinery's many products: gasoline, jet fuel, etc.

Dad was talking about the German battleship *Bismarck* and her destruction by the British Navy in World War II. I got interested and asked a few questions he couldn't answer. The following evening, he stopped by the RT library on his way home and checked out a copy of Winston Churchill's *Their Finest Hour,* a big red-covered, hardback volume of 500 or so pages. I started with the sections concerning the *Bismarck* and struggled through the entire book. Words, big and small, that I didn't understand, I asked about. When my parents got tired of answering me, I learned how to use the dictionary. In about three months I could read and read fast. The RT library became my hangout, where I gradually made my way through all six volumes of Churchill's World War II history. They were way more interesting to me than *Little Women*, the book my schoolteacher great-aunt back in the States had tried to use as a first reader. Sadly, Churchill didn't teach me to spell, and I still can't. Forty years later we found out that he made up a lot of the *Bismarck* story and left out the critical role played by the U.S. Coast Guard and the code breakers. I, for one, have reason to forgive him.

At about this time the Suez crisis of 1956 began when, responding to the nationalization of the Suez Canal, British, French, and Israeli troops invaded Egypt. We gathered around the radio every night at six p.m. to hear an Aramco employee read the Associated Press news. The strangest aspect of the experience for me was understanding that Dad wasn't rooting for the British but rather he favored the other side. He was justifiably worried about how the people of Arabia would react. I, however, was reading the Churchill books and thus thoroughly believed Britain stood for what was right in the world. History, of course, has sorted all this out, and is pretty much unanimous in condemning the invaders. President Eisenhower rose to the occasion; he was adamant that colonialism must end and threatened the U.S. tax deductions of Israeli charities. The invaders saw the wisdom of withdrawal. To me, it just might have been Eisenhower's finest hour.

• • •

The Ras Tanura senior staff school was much like Dhahran's, only better. Most important, for the first time in my life I was *known*. Our little Najmah community was composed of about 500 families with perhaps another hundred bachelors and bachelorettes. Thanks to Dad's work and Mom's singing, everybody knew them and—by association—me. As a result, there was considerable pressure on me to do well in school. My "acting up" just wasn't going to be risk-free anymore. Sadly, however, while you can take the boy out of the trailer park, you can't completely take the trailer park out of the boy. Several times as a Brat and many times since it has emerged.

Ras Tanura's Aramco's senior staff employees, and all Westerners, lived in Najmah. Most homes, like those seen above, were four-unit row houses. It was a small place, about 500 families and a hundred or so bachelors and bachelorettes. The large building in the background to the left is the school gymnasium where I played many games of basketball, the stands always full. To its right and even farther away are the theater and dining facilities. I believe Italian ex-POWs were the builders. You can see the Gulf in the distance. Our small home was out of the picture to the left.

Moving into our little Najmah row house in September 1956 seemed too good to be true. Our house, number 6128-1, was one of forty-four new units, built in what was then the farthest north area of the compound. It was less than 100 yards from the northern fence and even closer to the school, dining hall, theater, and beach. Why would you want to go anywhere else? If for some reason I did, there was a courtesy bus that circled and wove through the town, stopping wherever you wanted, including the hospital, commissary, general offices, and the refinery gate. It ran every twenty minutes and completed the route in about fifteen. Another bus, on the hour, would take you to Dhahran from where you could access Khobar. (That Dhahran trip took a bit more than an hour, although if it was time for prayer, the driver would pull off the road, wash his hands with sand, spread a small rug, and prostrate himself toward Mecca. All of which I soon believed seemed reasonable and would add a good fifteen minutes to the trip.) If you wanted to wade through water four feet deep you could make your way around the fence to the north and into unlimited desert. If you wanted to examine the tank farm, you just walked south along the shore and around the refinery's fence where it ended at the water line. I did it all.

My room was about ten by twelve feet, the same size as my room in Glenshaw, Pennsylvania. At night, the flare on the giant Qatif oil field's gas-oil separation plant (GOSP) shone through my curtained bedroom window, giving me a perpetual nightlight. Aside from the occasional shamal, or northwesterly wind dust storm, things were almost perfect for this Brat.

BEFORE BRATDOM

Mom and Dad had classical birth-order personality traits. I do as well. In addition, financial insecurity left its mark on them both. In my case, reversal-of-fortune-induced financial insecurity just might be the most dominate aspect of my personality.

Mom, aka Marian Teeters, was the third of six children, all born in Chicago. Neither of her parents attended college. Her older sister (child number one) had significant familial responsibilities and went on to graduate from college. Her older brother had fewer responsibilities but considerable musical talent, something exhibited by all six children and at least partially inherited from their mother. He became a music professor, first at Juilliard and later at the University of Florida. Mom had spectacular musical talent but lacked educational drive. Pleading financial insufficiency, she dropped out of the University of Michigan midway through her third semester, where, lucky for me, she had met Dad. (I once saw her college transcript, and suffice to say her grades did not suggest assured eventual graduation.) The younger the child, the less parental attention and the more difficult life's road.

Also lucky for me, Mom's sister Betty (child number five) and her husband, Melvin Beland, swept me into their nuclear family and gave me continuing, sustaining affection both before and particularly over the many years after the crash.

Mom, the third of six children, grew up in Chicago in a musically gifted family. Her voice exercise was "Una voce poco fa," an aria from The Barber of Seville. Music was everything to her and she practiced her craft religiously. She constantly performed (to rave reviews) in both Arabia and before, for meager financial reward.

Back in Chicago, Mom performed at and worked for the Cosmopolitan School of Music. It was through that relationship (I was told years later by her older sister) that she was in charge of squiring the Trapp Family Singers when they came to Chicago in the mid-1940s. My birth in 1946, plus the early-1953 addition of Laurie and Eileen, my younger twin foster sisters, crimped Mom's musical career but didn't end it. In the year before we left for Arabia, for example, she had been on local Pittsburgh television at least twice, giving folk-song concerts while playing the Irish harp. Looking back, I doubt Mom earned much more than the cost of her instruments and travel, but artists have to do what artists have to do. Her vocal exercise was *"Una voce poco fa,"* an aria from *The Barber of Seville*. You'd think she'd have gotten tired of it; I certainly did. Once I asked her what the Italian words meant. "No idea. I just memorize and sing them," she answered. Somehow this trait clearly did not pass on to me.

In Arabia, Mom very quickly resumed giving concerts, the first one in late 1956. She was darn good and had a seasoned performer's way about her. She'd sing a song while playing the harp or other instrument, then she'd retune the instrument while introducing the next song. The audience loved it, and of course they were starved for entertainment in an Arabia that lacked television, with DVDs and streaming videos far in the future. Mom was even invited to sing at the big Holland Music Festival in Hilversum, Netherlands—which she did. The truth I took away from Mom's career was that singing was a rich person's recreational activity. If you are America's

Dad, the second of five children, grew up in Bridgton, Maine. He had some rough edges, but by the time I was old enough to remember things he had sold his motorcycle and mellowed, at least superficially. Dad was a catapult officer on an escort carrier during World War II and scarred by his experiences.

10,000th best thirty-year-old accountant, you can have a good life. If you are the tenth best thirty-year-old female singer? Bah, and you'd better have a degree so you can teach. Mom, like so many talented poor kids, chased the nearly impossible dream.

Dad, aka Lewis Page Howard, was second in a family of five children born in the little town of Bridgton, Maine. The family was poor but not destitute, thanks to their frugality and hard work, which largely offset the disasters that befell his father, Laurence. (Laurence's mom died when he was three, his dad died when he was twelve, forcing him to drop out of school, and the 1919 agricultural commodity recession hit just as the family farm had expanded.) This was a family that knew reversal of fortune. Thanks to the sacrifices of her extended family,

Dad's mom, my grandmother Ruth Lewis Howard, was a Bates College graduate. The topic the year she was the captain of the debate team? Should women have the right to vote.*

There were books in Dad's home, and all three brothers were outstanding students and college graduates. They also all worked overseas at some point in their lives. Arthur, Dad's brother older by eighteen months, was smart, so Dad had to be smarter. (And as his son, I had to be smarter still.) A career foreign service officer, Arthur was diplomatic and conciliatory, so Dad had to be aggressive and challenging. I could go on. There was shared affection among the five children, but it's clear to me where Dad established that he was never going to meekly take orders from just anybody.

With financial help from the U.S. Navy, Dad paid his own way to an accelerated University of Michigan aeronautical engineering degree. He went right into the war in the Pacific and, lucky for me, survived. Four of his shipmates died in a kamikaze attack, and there were pilots he saluted as their planes catapulted off his escort carrier who did not return. Dad was scarred by the war

---

* I spent the summer of 1955, while Dad was by himself in Arabia, with my Howard grandparents. Laurence and I worked cutting and delivering wood most days. His view was that women voting, particularly when they weren't property owners, was just about the worst thing that had ever happened to America. I noticed, however, that he never expressed that view within earshot of his wife. When it came to the question of educating women and their role in politics, Dad had exposure to polar opposite views.

and never volunteered information about his experience. Any questions I asked were dismissed abruptly. He did stridently and continually advise—*never be a pilot*. Regardless, the war broadened his horizons. When he came back to America in December 1945, jobs were scarce, and he did not have a career to come back to. He was lucky to get low-paying work in Camden, New Jersey, as a safety engineer at Liberty Mutual Insurance. It must have been a brutal downgrade in responsibility.

I joined the family nine months after Dad's return, the three of us living together in a twenty-two-foot-long secondhand homemade trailer. When I was two, Dad got a similar job at Dravo, the big river barge and towboat builder, in Pittsburgh. We moved there and into two more trailer parks. For six years I slept on the trailer's lowered dining table, which certainly qualifies me as "trailer trash" although I also admit to having white privilege. My memories of the third park, in Butler, Pennsylvania, are quite vivid and not particularly pleasant. I will say that there were plenty of good people to be found there and everywhere we lived. I will also say that families living in houses near trailer parks often do not want their children associating with trailer trash. This point was brought home to this five-year-old by a playmate's mother, who screamed at me to never play with her son again and never enter their yard.

Just before I started first grade, we moved to a small three-bedroom home in the Pittsburgh suburb of Glenshaw. The trailer park frugality had netted my parents' savings just enough to cover the minimum down payment, and I believe Dad used a veteran's mortgage. Fall

I started life in a 22-foot second hand homemade trailer. We lived in three different parks, the first in Camden, New Jersey. Thirty-five years after leaving, I retraced my steps to within a mile of where we lived. At that point the area's ambience suggested discontinuing my memory-lane trip.

weekends were spent covering the house in the cheapest paint available: Dragon's Blood Red. Finances were tight, and my parents constantly fought over spending small sums, including one battle royal over stopping or not stopping to buy Tastee Freez ice cream cones. After the house and car payments, Mom had $22 a week for food and all other expenses. I was clothed in hand-me-downs and church-rummage-sale donations. (Note to my future great-grandchildren: Never give a six-year-old boy socks for Christmas, no matter how much he needs them. He will not remember you fondly.)

At some point, things got modestly better. Early the following year, 1953, we picked up three-year-old Laurie and Eileen at a multi child foster home. The twins had suffered difficulties with an older child, and when they entered our car, their fear of me was quickly apparent. I tried immediately to entertain them, while Dad and Mom explained that I was their new big brother, and it was my job to be their protector—a responsibility this six-year-old boy took very much to heart. The foster care institution provided payments that completely supported the girls. The plan was to have them in foster care, and if all went well after a year or two, proceed to adopt them. I was ecstatic. Four houses away and across the street, my new friend Glen had a baby sister; being a big brother was exactly what I wanted. (By the way, Glen's mom would read *Caesar and Christ* by Will Durant to the two of us. I owe my original interest in history to her.)

From my point of view, things went very well. I was assigned duties and was in charge of the twins when

Early in 1953 I acquired twin foster sisters: Eileen and Laurie. Being a big brother was something I wanted more than anything in the world. As a result of Dad losing his job, Foster Care took the girls from us eighteen-plus months later. Unreasonably, I never forgave my parents for this, particularly my mother.

Mom and Dad were out. My only painful babysitting memory was the time Eileen got herself locked in a neighbor's bathroom and couldn't get out. Eventually I got a small kitchen knife and, after jiggling it in the doorknob, freed the lock—a skill I used many years later in Beirut. After my initial shyness and their fear, the three of us were affectionate and loving toward one another, and I remember making up ridiculous stories involving the girls as princesses and myself as a knight. But the twins never got adopted. One day, early in my third-grade year, I came home from school and both girls were gone. We had been siblings for slightly more than eighteen months. Mom's explanation was terse: "They took them." She had nothing more to say and refused answering my shocked questions. There is no doubt that I never forgave my parents, particularly my mother, for the twins' departure. She had been home; she should have physically resisted.

Gradually and over the many years since, I gained a more reasonable understanding of what happened. The short version: Dad's candor had cost him his job, and losing the twins was just one of the serious ramifications. He absolutely had to get another position, and soon; budget fights intensified. He filled out endless forms in response to job postings. Foster Care didn't like the looks of a family without income and had quickly taken the twins from us. Dad needed a job for us to get them back. Further, Foster Care was leery of letting their charges move out of Pennsylvania, but the first reasonable employment opportunity was a safety engineering post with a chemical company in Baton Rouge, Louisiana. Dad was eventually rejected for the job, an outcome I feel I deserve a great deal of credit for—just as we approached the office building for his interview, I vomited orange soda all over him. There was no disguising the smell. The second hot prospect was with the Grand Coolie Dam in Washington State. I was not able to sabotage this opportunity, and Mom and Dad decided to accept the offer. They spent an evening telephoning all their friends with the news. The next morning's mail brought a job offer from Aramco, and after a few hours of intense discussion, they called the same friends again with the news that we were headed, instead, to Arabia.

The Aramco decision pretty much ended any hope that the twins would be part of my life going forward. Nobody was going to let foster parents adopt two little girls and take them to Arabia. I didn't understand this at the time, but my parents clearly did. It crushed me. Nine months later, my little sister, Beth, was born. I vowed I'd be the greatest big brother in history, almost certainly in response to the loss of the twins, and I usually came close. I didn't forget the twins, however. Thirty months later, in the summer of 1957, we were back vacationing in Pittsburgh and seeing friends, selling our house, and generally tying up loose ends. We had a free day and Dad made the mistake of saying we could use it to do anything I wanted. I said I'd very much like to see Laurie and Eileen. Bless his heart, he tried to make it happen. Despite a discouraging conversation with their grandparents, who now had custody, we drove to their home. No one answered when we rang the doorbell, but two little faces peered from between the curtains of an upstairs window. It was the last time I saw the twins and the only time I ever saw my father cry.

VACATION MEMORIES

10

Visit an Aramco expat of any vintage, and there's a reasonable chance you will see a map of the world on their wall. Countries, or perhaps cities, visited will be "pinned" or otherwise identified. (I am at fifty-five country visits and still counting.) In the 1950s and 1960s, a stint with Aramco was an opportunity to see the world and it still is, although with today's cheap airfares that's not quite the unique attraction it once was. Dad had spent much of WWII "seeing the sea," as he put it. But he had also been on the Philippine Island of Luzon, far removed from the capital city of Manila, for about three months at the end of 1945, and he definitely wanted to explore more foreign lands. Starting in the summer of 1956 with the Crusader castles trip, the Howards went on some great vacations, all carefully planned with built-in cost and travel-delay contingencies. Rather than hotels, we almost always stayed at low-priced pensions, the Airbnbs of the day. Dad constantly tried to line up local engineering professionals and their families for us to meet. Although I understood my role was to be seen and not heard, I was often brought into conversations and learned a lot by listening. Our family vacations were great trips to many interesting locations, but it is always the first of unusual experiences and trips that remain foremost in one's mind. Beyond the two trips already covered, a few later specifics demand recalling.

• • •

Before one trip, in 1957, Dad corresponded with the head engineer of the Dutch agency responsible for managing the dikes that kept below-sea-level Netherlands inhabitable. That engineer met us in the city of Lelystad, itself on land totally reclaimed from the sea, and spent a day in the car with us. Dad's enthusiasm and engagement were infectious, motivating that engineer, and usually most professionals we met, to tell him "everything." It was a life lesson that I carried over into my work as an investment analyst. Since we apparently "didn't want Beth with us" (my parent's words), she was left for a week in an Amsterdam nursery school where no one spoke English. Of course, at age twenty-three months, she didn't either. Regardless, I was appalled. But not appalled enough to stay with her and miss the excursion, not that I was given that option. When we came back for her, it was my neck that she clung to fiercely.

On the same vacation, we spent a morning at the Aalsmeer Flower Auction, the biggest in the world. The building, one of the largest in the world, held flowers flown in from seemingly everywhere. The three of us took in several rooms strewn with beautiful flowers. After about five minutes boredom set in, whereupon Dad parked me at the back of a huge adjoining room and said, "Don't move, we'll be back in two hours." It was more fascinating than I could possibly have imagined. There was what appeared to be a large clock on one wall that faced seating arranged in a semicircle, stadium style. At first, I didn't understand what was happening. The crowd pulsated with tension. Why did the clock's lone hand rapidly drop, counterclockwise, from 12 to 6? I was watching a "Dutch auction." The heavyset man sitting next to me chewing on an unlit cigar occasionally punched a button. Seeing my long period of rapt attention, he explained the system. Lots, containing hundreds to even thousands of

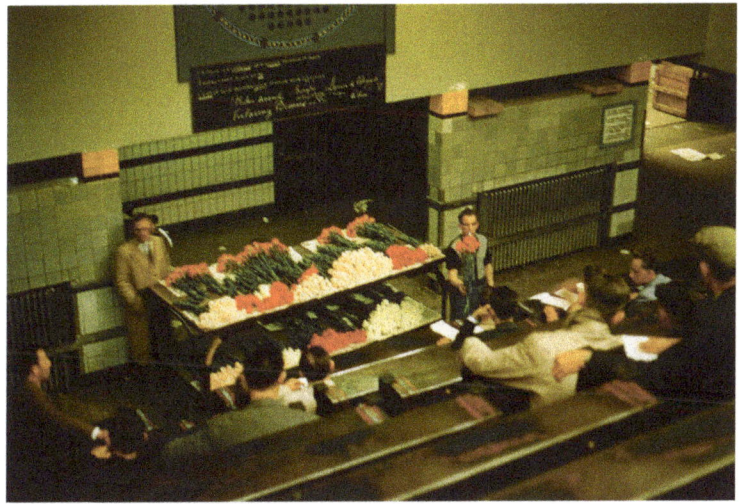

The Dutch Aalsmeer flower auction. The "clock's" one hand dropped from 12 to 6. The longer you waited to bid, the lower your purchase price, but the less likely you were to win. While I watched the action, Mom and Dad went sight-seeing through buildings equivalent in size to five football fields, holding flowers from all around the world. Today the bidding is computerized, but in essence unchanged.

individual flowers, were being sold to whoever hit the button first. Each tenth of a second reduced the price but also reduced your chance of being the winning bidder. The flowers were perishable and needed to be sold quickly. A standard auction with steadily rising bids would be too slow. My seatmate had scouted out the lots he wanted and had a shopping list with "buy" prices. He was a wholesaler to hundreds of retail shops. Mom and Dad came back in ninety minutes. They were worried that I'd be bored; I could have stayed all day. My primary interest as a ten-year-old was the movement of money between people. In later years I've often asked myself: Was the flower market a successor of Tulipmania? Now that is a story all investors should study.

• • •

Dad was a bargain hunter, and he had an easy rapport with pretty much everyone. He and the Kanoo Travel Agency in Khobar quickly found each other, and we enjoyed the fruits of last-minute bargains. The one I remember most vividly began one early morning in 1959, predawn in the Dhahran airport, and ended about thirty hours later in Paris, France. Our TWA flight made eight intermediate stops: Abadan, Iran; Basra and Bagdad, Iraq; Beirut, Lebanon; Istanbul, Turkey; Athens, Greece; and Rome and Milan, Italy. Mom called our trip the "milk run" and wasn't too happy about it. Even I, who got off in three previously unvisited countries, was downright worn out by the end. It was a last-minute Kanoo bargain opportunity that got my family on the fateful PIA flight.

On one return trip to the States in 1959, the Howard family traveled on the S.S. *America,* one of the last big ocean liners owned and operated by a U.S. company, which during the war had carried servicemen to and from the fighting in Europe. We boarded in Southampton, England, and stopped at Le Havre, France, before heading to New York. It crossed the Atlantic in six and a half days. Dad had splurged and we were in second class, enjoying waiters and white tablecloths. I got to see the

The floral clock on the lakefront in Geneva, Switzerland, was impressive, but what I most remember from that visit was entering my parents' hotel room and seeing a pile of revolver ammunition. Several years later we were again in Geneva. This time, in response to friction between King Saud and Crown Prince Faisal, there was consensus that Saudi Arabian paper money was doomed. Dad fitted me out with a money belt to carry wads of the currency into KSA surreptitiously. When the dust settled, Saud and Faisal reached an accommodation, and my life as a "mule" was stillborn.

last of a dying industry as much faster airplane travel was gradually driving the great liners out of business. Arabia wasn't the only thing changing.

At the end of that vacation, while heading back to Arabia from the United States, we stopped in Geneva, Switzerland. This trip was memorable for the beautiful floral clock by the lake and for a chance entrance into my parents' adjoining hotel room. On the table was a carry-on-bag-size pile of revolver ammunition. Dad, not pleased that I'd entered without knocking, explained it nonchalantly: "I'm taking that in for a friend." When I asked about customs, he said that it wouldn't be a problem and gave me the "shut up" look.

• • •

Arabia wasn't halfway around the world from Pittsburgh, but it was near enough that an around-the-world trip was financially feasible. (Aramco provided a travel allowance for each member of the family to return every two years to where the employee had been prior to being hired.) In 1961, Dad's little brother, Robert, was teaching at a missionary school in Kyoto, Japan; why not head there and continue across the Pacific to the States? So we did, stopping first in Hong Kong, where a tailor made my first suit—in three days (I wouldn't wear it for another sixteen months). Tokyo, Mount Fuji, and Kyoto were spectacular, but the gold medal experience goes to visiting the home and family of one of Robert's students. We were invited to lunch, and at one point, I wandered into a small room with lighted incense. On the wall was a portrait of a dashing young naval officer, an older son who had been killed when his destroyer had been sunk by U.S. aircraft near the end of World War II. Think about that for a minute or longer—I certainly did and have; it put a whole different light on what Dad had been part of. Killing people is not pretty, and while not relevant to investing, I have been something of a peacenik ever since.

HOWARD FAMILY ARAMCO DEITIES

In my opinion, Saudi Aramco today is the greatest industrial enterprise in the world. It gushes taxes to its host country and dividends to its owners (largely the government) as it gushes crude oil and refined products around the globe. Its oil field reservoir management skills lead the world. Its top staff is almost entirely Saudi citizenry, as are the bulk of its employees. American technicians, along with many skilled Saudis, fill middle management, a meritocracy with the occasional Pakistani engineer, Norwegian marine pilot, British security expert, Indonesian geologist, or other nationality added to the mix. You would never know, visiting Aramco today, that seventy-five to eighty years ago, only 100 American men held all the key jobs and that they and 1,000 Saudis kept the whole enterprise functioning while World War II raged. When my days as an active Aramco Brat ended with the crash in 1965, Saudis were beginning to move higher in management, but this was still a predominantly American-run company.

Plenty of observers find fault with Saudi Arabia today, while only a few seem able to recognize the powerful truth of Aramco's and the country's amazing transformation. Sixty-five years ago, about 40 percent of the company's Saudi employees could not read. Technology adoption throughout the country was essentially at medieval levels. Aramco's managerial and other capabilities far exceeded those of the KSA government. Things we take for granted—like roads, hospitals, telephones, and electricity—were likewise virtually nonexistent. Was the transformation made possible by oil wealth? Absolutely, but it didn't have to happen. Think of the resource-rich developing countries that have gone nowhere in the years since World War II. The obvious actor deserving most credit for the successful transformation is the Saudi government, or more accurately the ruling family. The country has had some spectacularly good kings over the past 119 years. Far more years of good leadership than the United States has had years of good presidents.

Another factor was national historic memory. The original Saudi state that covered nearly the whole Arabian Peninsula was smashed by the Egyptian army between 1802 and 1818. (Ruthlessly, the date palms were chopped down and the water wells filled in.) After a painful rebuilding, it next fell apart due to family bickering in the late 1880s. Nobody wanted to see a repeat of those disasters. A third factor was the inherent goodness of the people, untainted by the scourge of colonialism as the center of Arabia was too poor and remote to attract predators. The fourth factor, and essential in my view, was the Americans who came to Arabia to work in the oil industry. Because of their isolation and their typically long periods of employment, and because there was no one American owner of Aramco, they became Aramcons. They either soon stopped identifying with distant American companies or, like Dad, never did. Many were committed to the development of the Saudi employees who replaced them and gloried in the company's progress in this regard.

There are two, and to my knowledge only two, reminders of Aramco's American past in plain sight as one walks around Dhahran, the headquarters town, today: Hamilton House and Steineke Hall. Both are guest accommodations, originally built, I believe, by Italian ex-POWs. Dad never met either Lloyd Hamilton or Max Steineke, but he knew plenty of people who had, and he wasn't shy about

Dad spoke reverently about Max Steineke. His carefully located shallow wells were a brilliant and cheap way to create a structural understanding of eastern Arabia. This understanding in turn led to the discovery of some of the world's greatest oil fields.
(Photo courtesy of Saudi Aramco.)

passing judgment: Hamilton was a pretty good lawyer, representing Standard Oil of California, who happened to be in the right place at the right time. Specifically, when the original concession agreement allowing oil activities to begin in KSA was drawn up. Steineke, on the other hand, was a God, the greatest oil finder of all time. Dad credited him with discovering the super-giant oil fields: Ghawar, Abqaiq, Qatif, and even Safaniya.*

The key was drilling relatively inexpensive and shallow 600-feet-deep "information wells" in a carefully chosen and accurate grid pattern—all in the featureless desert. The data obtained served to deduce deeper underlying rock structures. That information, in turn, had the potential to indicate the possible location of crude oil accumulations. Steineke, and the men who followed him, drilled and found oil in enormous quantities. I can't say I understood Dad's thinking back then. But in later years, his conviction provided me a head start in understanding oil exploration fundamentals.

To find current evidence of the second Howard family deity of my Brat days, you must visit the Saudi Aramco Community Heritage Gallery at 12th Street and Ibis Avenue, Dhahran (or at least you could in 2019, when I was last there). Memorabilia as well as books by Aramcons and about Arabia fill the shelves. On one wall is a picture of the Aramco-built first girls' school in Saudi

---

* If you want a non technical introduction to Steineke's approach and successes, I recommend Michael Quentin Morton's book *Empires and Anarchies: A History of Oil in the Middle East.*

Safaniya, the world's largest offshore oil field, was found after Steineke left Aramco, but using his insights. In 1956 the jack-up rig that drilled the discovery and producing wells docked on the Tarut Bay side of Ras Tanura. Dad, as district safety engineer, had access to pretty much everything and he and I toured the rig alone. It was called a jack-up as it had three huge steel legs that were lowered to the sea floor once it was properly in location. Before actual drilling began, the rig was "jacked up" on those legs about twenty feet above the water. Each leg was lined with a series of impressive gear teeth to facilitate this movement.

Arabia; more on that in a few pages. On the opposite wall are the portraits of Aramco's past presidents, among them Thomas C. Barger. Barger had done fieldwork with Steineke, become proficient in Arabic, and grew with the company. My understanding is that one of his proposed local community-improvement projects was opposed based upon the reasoning of others in management that "Aramco was in the oil business." His rebuttal: "Aramco is in the business of maintaining the concession" (specifically, the legal agreement that allowed Aramco to operate in KSA). That thinking, the June 1956 strike (see footnote page 28), and the abysmal living conditions for Saudi workers outside the security gate resulted in the Saudi employee home-purchase program. More important to me, in September 1957, he transferred Dad to that program as Home Ownership Field Representative, Ras Tanura. Before leaving the subject of Tom Barger, I want to note that as president of the company he wrote me a quiet letter of sympathy dated June 1, 1965. In it he characterized my family as people all would be proud to call friends. He nailed it.

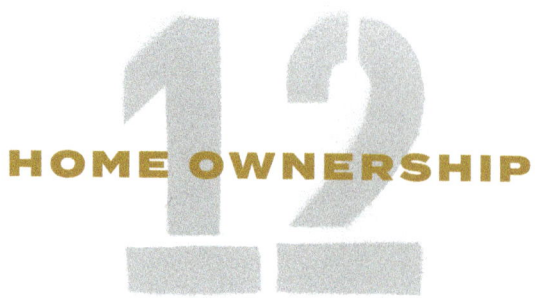

HOME OWNERSHIP

After a relatively unrewarding thirty months as a safety engineer, starting in September 1957, Dad began his Home Ownership assignment. More important, he continued to be eager to do things with me. We rose early on a typical Thursday morning (the first day of my weekend and his half day) and set off for Rahimah, Ras Tanura's new bedroom community for the Saudi employees of Aramco. It was planned for west of the general camp, on the other side of the road coming from Dhahran. We parked about fifty feet away from a house under construction. I was an eleven-year-old with a watch, a clipboard, and a pencil. My instructions were simple: count the bags of cement put in every time the concrete mixer is loaded, time the mixing before the concrete is unloaded, and keep track of slump tests. "Okay, but what is a slump test?" I asked. Dad explained: An open bucket is filled with the newly mixed concrete and then quickly turned and set upside down. Then the bucket is removed. Properly mixed concrete will maintain the shape of the bucket but "slump" a few inches. Overly mixed or watery material will run all over the place. "Okay, but aren't the workers going to change their behavior with me watching?" was my second question. Dad didn't think so. "You're just a kid sitting in a car. Two minutes after I leave, they won't even know you're here." And sure enough, he was totally right ... or at least I think he was since I never recorded an instance of substandard concrete preparation. But then again, maybe my presence did change their behavior.

Construction was simple enough to understand. Trenches for concrete footings were dug by shovel in the sand, with extra thickness and depth at the corners. Next, wooden forms (to hold the wet concrete) and steel rebar were placed before concrete was poured in. Once this had

Dad oversaw Rahimah, handing every aspect of the town. This was Ras Tanura's suburb for the Saudi employees of Aramco. Here, a typical house under construction with reinforced concrete and concrete block predominating. The only modern equipment used: a cement mixer.

set, concrete block was laid with appropriate openings for windows, doors, the occasional mid-wall structural support, and corners. After the first-floor block was in place, forms were fitted such that all was bound together, including the top of the block wall, with another pour of concrete strengthened by rebar. Next came the floor of the second story, all reinforced concrete. After that, the second story is done in a similar manner to the first, and then finally, the roof (with a parapet wall) and the floor of the lower story. Most of the labor required to build these houses was unskilled, the concrete mixer was the only modern equipment, and it was easy to manage. I suppose by today's standards this was a pretty inefficient way to build a house, but it worked.

Where was Dad going while I watched the workers? His little town had serious problems. In fact, it was just a small grid layout of streets with a few houses. It didn't look at all like a town to him. There had been no thought of expansion. There was no long-term plan for schools, utilities, traffic patterns, or mosques. More immediate problems were corruption, shoddy work, and financial abuses—a lot of problems that all had to be simultaneously attacked. And attack them he did.

Obvious corruption was easier to spot and unravel than you'd think. The "bad actor" contractors were quick to give Dad gifts: gold watches and Persian rugs were typical. Some of these he brought home to show us, returning them the next day. He investigated contractors that had thereby identified themselves, and it usually took less than a week to figure out what each was doing. The corruption strategy I remember best was simple. An employee would take out a loan of say $7,600 for an $8,000 house. The contractor would build a $3,000 house. Maybe use half the normal cement in the concrete, skip rebar in the footings, the sort of quality shortcut that could be hidden. Contractor and employee would then split the $5,000 differential. Finally, after a month or two, the employee would decamp for parts unknown, defaulting on the loan. A system of inspections and related progress payments went a long way toward solving this problem. Hence my time with the watch and clipboard. Initially, Dad had one American and four Saudi inspectors. He claimed that the one American added only 2.5 percent to the cost of each of his houses, while adding expertise that dramatically boosted the quality of his total inspection effort. He was always trying to get a Saudi college student as a summer intern inspector, but I don't know if that ever happened. Eventually a very competent Saudi named Mubarak became his right-hand man, replacing the American. You'll briefly meet Mubarak again in a few pages.

You'd think that timing concrete mixers for Dad and visiting water wells and sewage treatment plants with him wouldn't have interested me, but you'd be wrong. The Imhoff sewage treatment plant, with its 1906 technology, is the outing I remember best. Smelly sewage flowed into one large concrete vat, settled, and gradually entered a second vat. There it was "digested," lost its smell, and became sludge. Dad had plans for mixing that sludge with sand to create a growing medium (soil) for the trees and bushes he wanted in the public places. They would be watered by the plant's liquid runoff. I shudder to think of the health risks all this would have engendered.

But modern technology has largely and safely achieved the results Dad wanted back then. (Sadly, when I visited Rahimah in 2019, there was little evidence of public greenery, although I suspect it can be found behind the walls of individual houses.) Without a doubt, these outings were a fantastic introduction and preparation for my professional career as a securities analyst. The terminology was different, but it was only a small intellectual step from understanding the basic underpinnings of Rahimah to the basic underpinnings of a public company's business model. That investors need to understand business models seems old-fashioned in the financial euphoria of the soaring 2021 bull market, but it won't when the inevitable stock market decline comes along.

House plans were always being considered as we sat down to our evening meals. Dad wasn't happy with the designs being built, although in the end he accepted plenty of their features. He wrote request letters to oil companies and government organizations in Kuwait, Iran, and India, and those were just the ones he told me about. Most were proud to send him their best house plans. In addition, handbooks of all sorts began arriving: *Building Construction Handbook*, *Design*, and *Civil Engineering* were the ones I remember and just the tip of the iceberg. He wrestled with three key differences between a Saudi home and American one. First of all, his homes had to be designed for at least eight people, maybe more. An Aramco employee typically wanted at least four children and was likely to have his parents, possibly his in-laws, and maybe even a younger sibling living with him. Our Saudi employee had much more income than anyone else in the Arabian society, and he was expected to take care of his extended family. Second, while there might be small bedrooms, most sleeping was done communally on the roof. It seldom rained in Arabia, and of course the roof was much cooler than inside the house at night. Third, Dad's houses had to provide for likely gender separation and exclusion of sexes from certain areas.

In the early days, employees working at other Aramco locations never chose to build in Rahimah, but those working in Ras Tanura often had reason to build in the Dhahran area or the nearby Qatif Oasis. Both those locations were more established communities with a pedestrian flavor. Dad and his inspectors were responsible for all RT employee houses. Qatif, in particular, was attractive if you had family living there, and initially about one-quarter of the RT employees' homes were built there. Accompanying Dad on a site visit once, I found the oasis fascinating. The employee's father's home was next door and he invited us in for tea. The father was a man of property; he owned forty date palms. Harvest economics were elegant capitalism at its best. Pollinators and harvesters, both of whom had to climb the trees, each got a set percentage of the revenue. Also paid was the water supply and the team who processed the dates by basically rotating them in the sun over several days. Our host, the tree owner, got a set percentage as well. A bad harvest and everybody suffered. A good harvest and everyone fared well. All are committed to success. It reminded me of a visit I had to Mystic Seaport when I was six. Yankee whaling ships divided their haul with set fractional distributions to harpooners, lancers, blubber

Dates were the cash crop of the oasis of Qatif, along with subsistence agriculture. Modest amounts of sheep-herding took place in the surrounding desert. An Aramco employee's father explained to me how the date revenue was divided among pollinators, harvesters, tree owners, and the communal water supply.

cutters, sea captains, and shipowners. Activities that generated money and how that money was split between participants have always interested me.

Don't think that Qatif, with its grassroots, helter-skelter development, was better than Rahimah. It wasn't. It's natural from the vantage point of today to see a certain depressing sterility in a company town, but back then sterile was worth a lot. On the same visit mentioned above, we chanced upon a butcher shop selling a freshly slaughtered lamb. The hanging carcass was unrecognizable; a black sea of flies inches deep obscured its shape. Like Khobar at that time, Qatif had powerful smells and hygiene was lacking.

• • •

Although no longer in the safety sector, Dad was still called upon in that capacity, and he put himself at risk fighting the extremely dangerous refinery fires that occurred periodically. The most spectacular of these involved a 420,000-gallon propane tank that exploded with towering flames and heat I thought I could feel standing four miles away in the street outside our home in north Najmah. Mom and the other wives watched in barely concealed horror. Dad's clothes stank of petroleum when he came home.

Two days later he drove me through the refinery and showed me steel equipment that had been in proximity to the fire now nearly melted and sagging from the intense heat. The firefighters had worked while being drenched with water. Dad said it was fortunate that no one was killed. Later I realized that that included him. In writing this memoir, I have realized something else. Our drive through was absolutely forbidden and we were stopped about halfway through by a very upset security man. I strongly suspect that Dad was considering not only how to protect a refinery but perhaps also how to destroy it. Saying he wanted to show me the damage, and that I wanted to see it, was plausible deniability for him ... and it worked.

Refineries are inherently dangerous. Dad snapped this picture of what he considered "a small fire." It was the number two crude unit, and related damage repairs cost $250,000. Thanks to inflation and increased equipment sophistication, repair today would cost perhaps $5 million. When the 420,000-gallon propane fire occurred, he was too busy fighting it to be taking photos.

• • •

Meanwhile, Dad grew more and more focused on his town plan. He and his draftsman fretted over details as minor as curb heights, drainage grades, and speed bumps. Where to put telephone, electrical, and sewage lines were bigger questions. But the huge bone of contention was schools. Dad had decided early on that Rahimah would have both a boys' school and a girls' school. George Rentz and his staff at the Government Relations Department were not about to let something so dramatic upset their dealings with local officials. (There had never been a KSA girls' school.) Dad would have to change his plan—only he wouldn't. His fight-to-the-death position was simply stated: "The men raised here will be the next generation of Aramco's workers. They will be educated, and they will want educated wives." No matter how unequal an argument's participants, you can't count out an idea whose time has come. Government Relations caved, getting one significant concession from Dad. When he presented the plan to local officials, he would not mention either school, but instead talk in specifics about some common town elements and in generalities about others, while making sweeping gestures over the large-detailed blueprint. That

Under the auspices of Aramco, the first KSA girls' school was built by Dad in Rahimah. He fought long-standing traditions to make it happen. His argument: "The men raised here will be educated, and they will want educated wives." Today Saudi women outnumber men in pursuit of university degrees.

way, if there were an eventual backlash, almost everyone but Dad could plausibly claim that they hadn't realized a girls' school was included. Well, the plan, and with it the schools, was approved. The schools were built and no one objected, and Saudi Arabia began the slow essential progress toward eventually treating women as equals. There is plenty about Dad that doesn't "grade" excellent by today's standards, but building the girls' school certainly does. This was his finest hour.

13
THE THEATER BECKONS

Mom's first Aramco concert, held in late 1956, had not gone unnoticed, and in early 1958, she was asked to try out for a part in the local theater group's production of *South Pacific*. But why am I saying "asked" as if it were a close call? She probably knocked down any competitors at the casting call. Truthfully, no one could sing like she could, and she was forceful at demanding others recognize that superior talent. The part she wanted was the female lead, Nellie Forbush. The play is set during World War II on an island in French Polynesia, an environment, if not a specific locale, experienced by Dad and many other of Aramco's then employees. Forbush, a young Navy nurse of Southern provincial upbringing, falls for a French planter who has two adorable children by a deceased Polynesian mother. Racial prejudice and the gulf between officers and enlisted men are constant themes. Of course, Mom got the part.

The rehearsals went on for nearly six months, and while I liked the folk songs that were part of Mom's usual repertoire, these songs were ones you could sing, understand, and feel good about. Plus, no more indecipherable

Italian. The great thing about it, looking back, was doing something with Mom. My enthusiasm for reading, be it history, sports, or literature—especially Mark Twain—was never going to capture her attention. She wasn't interested in anything but music and hadn't grown up with parents who were involved with her or in her schooling—and she and Dad never helped me with mine. (I taught my sister everything I could think of, every chance I could. Later, my wife and I were very involved with our boys' schooling.)

In return, it was clear through my demonstrated lack of talent that I wasn't going to learn to play the piano or any other musical instrument. With *South Pacific*, however, we were on the same page. We practiced dialogue together, and by the dress rehearsal, I knew not only Mom's lines but those of every character she shared the stage with. Even today certain phrases occasionally slip into my conversation, and I often find myself singing or whistling one of the songs. "There is Nothing Like a Dame" remains a favorite, brought on whenever I prepare a mango (if you've heard the song, you understand).

Dramaramco was the wonderful name of the local theater group, and it is truly amazing how committed Aramco was to its support. Extracurricular activities, in those days, were thought to be a key to the morale and success of the company. Larry Barnes, an electrician who managed several of Mom's Irish harp concerts, noted that Aramco actually assigned an employee full time to keep the *South Pacific* production on track.* In total, about

---

* Taken from Larry Barnes's memoir, *Looking Back Over My Shoulder*, self-published in 1979.

THE THEATER BECKONS 103

Tobi
Marian Howard of Ras Tanura as Nellie Forbush and Lyman Rhodes of Dhahran as Emil deBecque are the stars of "South Pacific" which opens a five-night engagement at the Dhahran Theater tonight.

In 1958 Mom played the lead in the local theater production of South Pacific. *"Dusty" Rhodes was her co star. More than 300 members of the Aramco community performed or worked on some aspect of the show. This picture shared the front page of the October 15, 1958* Sun and Flare *(Aramco's newspaper) with a visit of the king and crude production reaching a record 1,08,000 barrels per day. It was not a slow news day!*

300 people performed in or worked on some aspect of the show, including an orchestra and a chorus. All these skills were found within our Aramco community, and just as important, vacation and work schedules needed to be arranged to accommodate its rehearsal and performance schedules—something only the company could do. (Can you imagine a profit-maximizing corporation today doing this? Not likely.)

I attended the dress rehearsal and one of the five evening performances. While it was unpleasant watching Mom, the convincing actress, getting romantically entwined with another man, the play was fantastic. The Aramco edition of *South Pacific* was my first live musical performance—indeed my first stage play—and it left me wanting more.*

---

* A few years later, when flying solo to and from high school in the United States, I would always try to stop in London to see a show. I never paid more than about 90 U.S. cents, always sitting in "restricted viewing" seats. My favorite London show? *Oliver*. My flight was delayed during one of my London stopovers, and when I arrived at my cut-rate airport hotel, where I had a reservation, there were no rooms available. The counter staff could see that I'd come on the terminal bus and hardly exhibited signs of affluence. After a hurried conversation, I was asked if sleeping on a rollaway in the ladies' coatroom would be acceptable. "Fine by me," I said and went right to sleep. The first few times when the attendant unlocked the door, turned on the light, and came in to get a coat, I woke up. But eventually I just slept right through the interruptions. This wasn't the first time in my young life that I'd relied on the kindness of strangers, and it wouldn't be the last. In Detroit I once spent a day walking and riding the bus

South Pacific and my exposure to other shows brought me into contact with a whole different set of people, both then and throughout my life. People who were educated and well-off, who spoke about interesting things and didn't use the vocabulary common in trailer parks and oil camps. Emotions, attitudes, and consequences I hadn't considered were on display. Through the theater, I glimpsed a different world from the one where I had been brought up.

---

so that I could see a matinee performance of *Peter Pan*. Mary Martin, the star in that show, had played Nellie Forbush in the original Broadway production of *South Pacific*. I wanted to see how she compared to Mom. Well, my totally biased opinion was that Mom was significantly better. Admittedly, playing *Peter Pan* may not have featured Martin's best romantic talents.

SCHOOL, SPORTS, AND SCOUTS

An amazing thing happened that first year in Ras Tanura: I didn't get sick. Surrounded as I was by water and desert, my undiagnosed pollen allergy simply vanished. (In Pittsburgh I had regularly missed fifty-plus days each school year. When I returned six years later to Michigan, I suffered sneezing but not the debilitating cold-like symptoms I once had.) Avoiding sick days was huge, but even more helpful to my schooling was a partial easing of my hostile attitude toward teachers. Class size in Ras Tanura (usually about twenty and eighteen in my ninth-grade year) was less than Dhahran, and although I was not a model student, my behavior didn't cause the same level of disruption it had there and in Pittsburgh.* Of course,

---

* I still had my moments, however. Consider the few sentences I wrote when assigned to create a story that featured a dog, a girl, and water. My protagonist, a five-year-old girl, spotted a dog urinating on the sidewalk. She said, "Look Mommy, dog water." Assignment fulfilled. When read out loud, class decorum pretty much destroyed for hours.

knowing how to read was also a big plus—and suddenly I regularly had grades between the middle and top third of my class. Another big positive was organized sports. With only six boys, it was difficult for our grade to compete with the other Aramco districts (for example, at that time, Dhahran School had about fifty boys and was able to field two teams, and Abqaiq had closer to ten). Hence, we were generally disadvantaged, but it was a great opportunity for me to participate athletically. From baseball to touch football to basketball, I played all sports well, at least against my particular competitors.

Looking back from the vantage point of today's mores and attitudes, the treatment of the girls in our class is downright embarrassing. They were expected to be cheerleaders or baton twirlers at our games, and seemingly no one (except some parents, I suppose) particularly cared about their schoolwork. Girls didn't cause trouble and therefore didn't get much attention—it was shameful. Chronically socially awkward, I had no appreciation for what a two-to-one girl-to-boy ratio must have meant to the girls. Plus, older boys were out of the picture. Aramco schools ended with the ninth grade and, assuming an employee stayed in Arabia, his children were sent out of the country for further education.

The Najmah/Ras Tanura community supported its students at every turn. Our junior high athletic events got press coverage. The town, with limited entertainment options, turned out for our games. Bachelors were often coaches or volunteer assistants on our sports teams. You had only to ask and support for a youth activity materialized. Through sports, I gained a presence in the community, and it forced me to behave and to strive to succeed. Recognition for my athletics fed my desire to do better in all things: school, sports, and scouts.

The most positive experience we had as a group in ninth grade was when all the boys played on our six-man touch football team. We won a single game, lost three, and tied two—perhaps our most successful athletic season. Our camaraderie continued haphazardly as we went on in life: six years later Joe, the center on our team, was wounded on the bridge of the U.S.S. *Liberty* when an Israeli torpedo boat and jets repeatedly attacked the ship in June 1967. He later earned an accounting degree, worked for Saudi Aramco, and became an advocate for the *Liberty*'s crew. Herb became a federal judge in Connecticut. Tom died young after working at a Shell refinery outside Saint Louis. Mike went to Kenyon College and at one point ran a language school in Kuwait. Alan, my best friend in Ras Tanura, scored 800 on his math SAT (his dad gave me a piece of advice that I followed faithfully throughout college and into my career: read the center two columns of the *Wall Street Journal*'s front page every day). I am proud to have been that group's quarterback.

In the late fall of 1960, that same ninth-grade year, a big unexpected academic improvement occurred. Beth was in kindergarten, which started fifteen minutes before my own classes, both in the morning and after lunch. Ever the big brother, I escorted her on the five-minute walk to school. Alan, who lived in the same alley, usually accompanied us. Unexpectedly, Jan, our class's top student, joined us for three weeks. Her parents had gone on vacation and left her with friends who also lived on our

SCHOOL, SPORTS, AND SCOUTS

eight-unit alley. Jan was a seismic event. She checked, first thing every morning, to see that we had done our homework properly. If I hadn't, she helped me get it done in the fifteen minutes before our classes started. If we were having a test that day, she'd prep me. She was organized and had all assignments and the related work planned out. Somehow, Jan got me working harder and smarter. I owe her.

Walking Beth to school continued through my ninth-grade year, the highest grade Aramco schools went to, and also when I returned to Ras Tanura during the summers that followed. I started another walking habit that year. By 1960, Dad had moved his office from inside the security fence to the middle of Rahimah. On Thursdays, if I was free, I would walk from our home to the pedestrian gate of the general camp, through the camp, and then about ten blocks to Dad's office. It was a straight shot, perhaps a bit more than a mile. I timed my trips to arrive around 11:30 a.m., which was half an hour before Dad was through for the week. He was often finished with pressing matters and would spend time discussing with me what he was working on. When the noon whistle blew, we would drive home, passing the old shack area, which was shrinking but not fast enough for Dad.

The other big activity that got me out of the Najmah compound was Boy Scouts and camping. My friends joined Scouts—so I did too—and what a good decision it was. Learning skills and putting them to use appealed to me. We'd read about a topic, say fire starting, in the *Scout Handbook*, and then we would practice in our back yards. Finally, a Scout leader would watch us each do the skill, often at a cookout, and sign our "Scout's Own Record" book. Camping, hiking, cooking, and assorted other outdoor skills engaged me.

Dad had not been a Boy Scout, but he quickly grew interested in my progress. By the time I earned my Tenderfoot and Second Class ranks at age twelve, he was the troop committee chairman, a post he would hold until he died. Dad continually came up with ways to encourage myself and others to advance. At one point this included an "honor trip" up TAP—the Trans Arabian Pipeline—for Scouts who had advanced a rank in the past year. We flew from the small airstrip in Ras Tanura to Nariya, a large pump station with overnight accommodations (we also used our tents).* From there we explored by Land Rover, notably nearby Ras al Mish'ab, on the Gulf where Aramco had established a residential camp when the pipeline was being built (Florence Chadwick worked and trained for her record-setting English Channel swim there in addition to

---

* Aramco aviation was a big deal. Saudi Arabia is the size of the United States east of the Mississippi. With poor to nonexistent roads, getting around the country was best by air, and pilots were valued employees. They were often called upon to ferry the king, and it is a treat at Aramco Brat reunions to hear the stories those men have passed on to their children. I believe the three DC-6s mentioned in chapter 2 took turns flying once a week to and from the States. Plus, there were two flights weekly to Asmara, Eritrea, to bring in produce for the company commissary (at that time, as a result of World War II and some very misguided thinking, Eritrea was part of Ethiopia). I have also recently learned that the U.S. Army/CIA maintained a well-guarded listening station in Asmara that monitored radio traffic throughout the region.

training at Najmah). By landing pipe at Mish'ab, you saved yourself a 200-mile road journey, but of course at first there wasn't a road or deep water near the shore. The latter problem was overcome by creating a giant imitation ski lift: a series of telephone poles that marched out a mile or two into the Gulf, with connecting cables (the poles were still in place when we visited in 1959, about a dozen years after they had been installed). Hearing about the TAP's construction was also interesting. Steel pipe, 30 inches in diameter, was shipped from the United States inside 31-inch diameter pipe, both 30-foot lengths (I assume the larger diameter were used on uphill stretches, where gravity adds to the challenge of moving the petroleum). After landing at Ras al Mish'ab, three sections were shop-welded into 90-foot lengths, thereby minimizing difficult field welding. Hearing the story of construction from men involved in running it and seeing the pipeline started me thinking I'd like to be a welding engineer.

Building the TAP was managed by Bechtel, or as it was known in Saudi Arabia, IBBI: International Bechtel Builders Incorporated. When completed, the 750-mile-long TAP was the longest pipeline in the world, moving about 330,000 barrels of crude every day to a tanker terminal in Sidon, Lebanon. From there the crude oil was shipped to refineries around the Mediterranean and even as far as Rotterdam, Holland. (It's an indictment of all involved that TAP doesn't operate today and hasn't since 1976.) Like many adolescents, I dreamed of being something important, and when I saw the IBBI engineers who visited RT wearing clean clothes and commanding attention, I thought, *I'll be that when I grow up.*

Another Boy Scout trip that Dad arranged took us to a small, one-family oasis inland from Jubail, a coastal town about 100 miles north of Ras Tanura. The oasis had been abandoned due to the steady encroachment of desert sand. Mubarak, Dad's right-hand man, came along with us, and I was intrigued by his camping equipment. Instead of a tent and sleeping bag, he brought a Persian carpet—when it was time for bed he just rolled up in the carpet. It kept him plenty warm, and the heavy dew didn't penetrate the tiny tight knots of wool. I suppose a random desert creature may have joined him for the night, but that could have happened no matter what your sleeping arrangements. At one campout, I awoke to find a young scorpion in my sleeping bag enjoying my body warmth. The only downside to the Persian rug was its weight; you wouldn't want to use it on camping trip that involved a hike.

We also visited a Bedouin encampment on another trip north. The Bedu father served us fresh goat's milk and tea. I was particularly impressed by his fire-making skills and his two-foot-deep hole in the sand that had struck water. How did he know where to dig? On that trip Dad was along, but when he or Mubarak weren't on Scout trips into the desert, the smattering of Arabic I'd acquired in Khobar was usually better than any of the adult leaders and I was the de facto translator for Saudi/Scout interactions. Sadly, in those days, not many of Aramco's American employees learned the language. That changed over the years ahead.

Closer to home, we Scouts often tented near the old Italian camp. By then I was earning money babysitting

On camping trips 40-plus miles from Ras Tanura, we Scouts often encountered Bedouin. These were invariably positive hospitality experiences, when we would be invited into the "male" tent accommodations and offered refreshment. In this picture, I'm in the shadows to the left and behind the Bedu, who has just gotten a crackling fire going using the scantiest of fuel. Small cups of cardamom flavored tea are brewing. Nearby is a newly scooped two-foot hole that somehow has found water for the tea and the Bedu's sheep. We scouts found the camping skills on display beyond impressive.

children my sister's age and spending it carefully on lightweight camping equipment. My complete kit weighed under twenty pounds, which meant I could easily carry an extra pack for a short distance if, as usual, one of our younger Scouts was having trouble on the five-mile hike. I always walked at the back of the troop to help stragglers. Further, since I could set up camp and get a fire going in about five minutes, I was available to help the less skilled in these activities. I loved it.

During ninth grade, I was the troop's senior patrol leader and was into accumulating merit badges, an activity I continued as a returning summer student. Cold-calling men I didn't know to set up meetings to review skills was necessary and hard even for me, but I did it. It was great preparation for the telephoning a security analyst must do when researching a potential investment. The one I remember most vividly was meeting with the hospital administrator for the public health merit badge. We talked about various required topics, including campout latrines, and then got into the problems he faced in Ras Tanura—among them mosquitos, flies, and locusts. He had managed the malaria eradication program some years earlier and was dealing with the ongoing trachoma problem (see chapter 3). I experienced locusts twice during those RT years, and as an adolescent I had fun eating grasshoppers lightly cooked in oil. He saw the use of DDT as extremely dangerous but essential to protecting the little bit of green we had around us. I don't know if he'd read Rachel Carson's book *Silent Spring*, which was published in June 1962, right about when we talked, but I do know that our wonderful cat died—poisoned by the insecticide used fighting the swarms. Hopefully the locusts I ate were not poisoned. If they were, no obvious ill effects have shown up.

By the time I was nearing the end of Scouting at age seventeen, I had become Ras Tanura Troop 2's first Eagle Scout. At one point, the Dhahran Troop hosted us at Half Moon Bay, a seaside location near their camp. We always paired with Scouts on campouts, and on this one I was the odd man out. Dhahran's Tim Barger, the president's son, was similarly "odd" and ended up being my tenting buddy. We had similar skills and set up a unique shelter combining our rain ponchos. Both then and later in life, he was a fun person to be with. It was hard to tell which pleased Dad more, the Eagle or tenting with Tim.

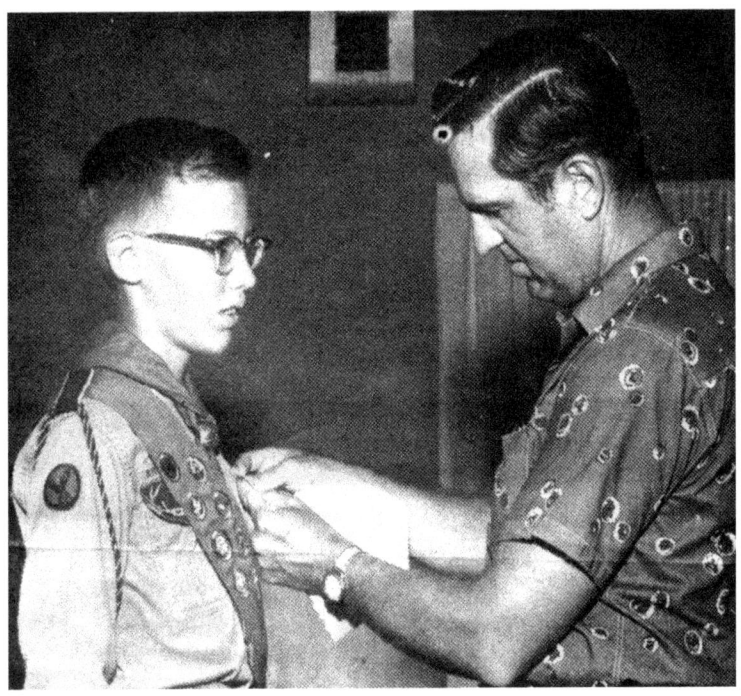

Receiving the Life Scout award at a Court of Honor ceremony in 1961 (photo from Sun and Flare*). Over the summers of the next three years I finished another eleven merit badges and became Ras Tanura's first Eagle Scout. The related 1965 ceremony was scheduled but never held due to the Cairo crash.*

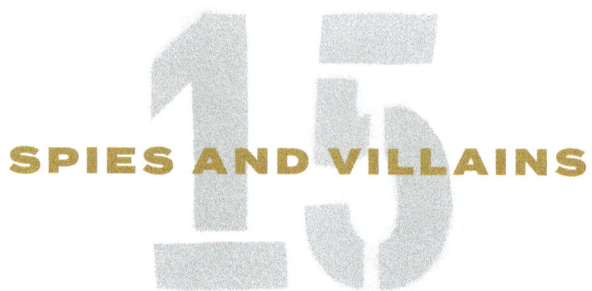

SPIES AND VILLAINS

In the summer of 1961, the Howard family was in the United States on a long vacation. While there, Dad arranged for us to visit Cranbrook School in Bloomfield Hills, Michigan. There we were given a tour by Harry Hoey, the headmaster whom you'll meet again later in this memoir. For now, however, I would be enrolling for tenth grade in ACS, the American Community School, in Beirut, Lebanon. But first I had to get there. Dad, Mom, and Beth took me to Idlewild Airport on Long Island, New York, for my send-off. I got kisses and great hugs from both Mom and Beth, and I forced a hug and kiss on Dad who wanted to just shake hands. The things we remember.*

KLM, the Dutch airline, flew me to Amsterdam for an overnight. I added further excitement to the trip by getting lost after dark while exploring a deserted, bombed-out section of the city. A very nice bus driver eventually

---

* This was the last time I kissed Dad and the last time I said "I love you." There were many missed opportunities in the three years ahead, and it is little consolation that Dad would never initiate or encourage affection. Not surprisingly, my two sons have had to endure constant barrages of "I love you" and numerous hugs.

picked me up; he didn't speak English but understood "Hotel Krasnapolsky." After shuttling passengers along his route, he drove me a good ten minutes out of his way to my lodgings. Twenty-four hours later I was at ACS.

Beirut in 1961 was, along with Berlin, Cold War central. World War II had been won by our oil producers (our military had ample fuel; the Nazis and Japanese were always desperately short) as well as on the battlefields. U.S. crude production was expected to peak by 1970, and the world's demand for Middle East oil was growing rapidly. Large producers Saudi Arabia, Iran, and Iraq were all considered as being at risk to Russian mischief, while Kuwait, Qatar, and the seven Trucial States (now the UAE) were such small political entities as to be vulnerable to all manner of threats.

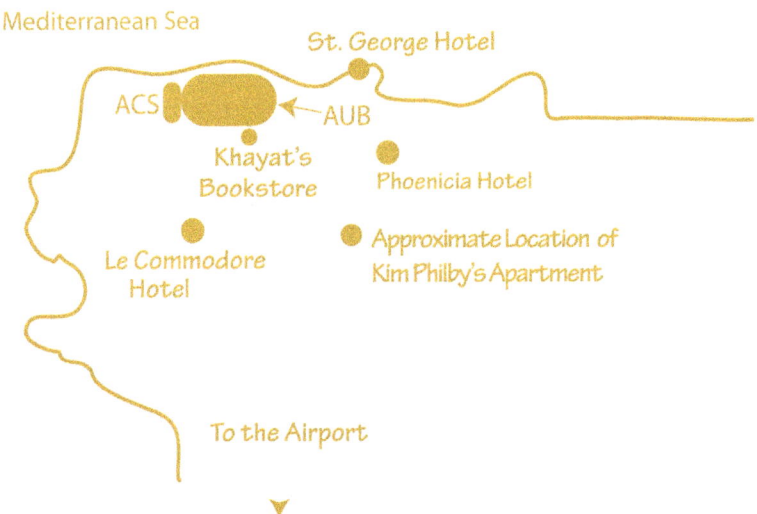

DOWNTOWN BEIRUT - 1961
(AUB Campus is about 1/4 by 1/2 mile)
ACS American Community School
AUB American University Beirut

Today we recognize that the United States merits only modest moral high ground in the Cold War played out in the Middle East, given our involvement in the 1953 coup d'état that toppled Iranian Prime Minister Mosaddegh. I'm also suspicious that the CIA may have played a role in a Syrian regime change a few years earlier (TAP, that pipeline I'm so proud to have visited, wasn't getting Syrian approval until the coup d'état). It was no coincidence that Englishman Kim Philby, probably history's most successful spy, was last posted in Beirut before escaping to Moscow. He had an apartment in the Qantari area, convenient in one direction to Le Commodore Hotel favored by journalists (and perhaps spies?), and in another direction to the Saint George and Phoenicia hotels. The bars, pools, and especially the reception areas of the latter two were an obvious attraction to the movers and shakers of the otherwise puritan Middle East. He also had an entree to important Arabs through his father, a longtime advisor to the KSA royal family. (Although father Philby had criticized that family's extravagances once too often.) During the year, Philby and I were both in Beirut and often frequented the same locations. I like to think that on occasion we were unknowingly in the same room together, but that's probably just an enjoyable fantasy.

Local stresses added to Beirut's international tensions. Lebanon, as a country, was less than twenty years old, having gotten rid of French colonial control during World War II. The country was about half Christian and half Muslim, plus it had a large number of displaced Palestinian refugees. The Muslim population itself was splintered, not only by Sunni and Shia, but also by lesser-known subsects such as Druze and Isma'ili (a group originally known as Assassins) that confused me at the time and to some extent still do. Bottom line, there was nothing like a "loyal opposition" attitude by any of those who were out of power toward those in power. They each sought dominance and grew steadily more ruthless in its pursuit. Within fifteen years of my attending ACS, a civil war had broken out, and the perceived tranquility of Beirut would be irretrievably shattered by the murder of Malcolm Kerr, the president of AUB, the American University of Beirut. (Basketball fans will recognize Kerr's son Steve, former ACS student, NBA player, and now coach of the Golden State Warriors.) The American Community School, both then and throughout its existence, was adjacent to AUB, in the heart of the action.

You had only to walk fifty feet from the dorm's front gate to find a three-card monte game. It was fascinating to watch and see how the outsiders were fleeced by the insiders. The shills were very convincing, and I once watched as one of them gave up his watch before winning and getting it back. I was never tempted to play; bent card corners had a way of disappearing when things truly counted. Past that activity and up three flights of stone steps would get you near the university bookstore, Khayat's. It sold switchblades, whips with hidden knives, and blackjacks. Paul, the owner, could get you a revolver but probably wouldn't provide a silencer. Everything, and I mean everything, was for sale in Beirut in 1961.

Early in my time at ACS, a Ras Tanura friend of my parents arrived in Beirut for a holiday. She didn't have a child attending the school but thought perhaps the five of us RT Aramco Brats would like to go out with her for a nice early-evening meal at an upscale restaurant on the coast south of town. Did we ever—dining hall food left a lot to be desired. She arrived with two taxis, one for herself and two of the girls, and one for myself, the other boy, and a third girl. We had a wonderful meal, played a word-spelling game I found stupefying, and piled into our separate taxis to head back to Beirut.

There had been changes while we were at dinner. Near the Palestinian refugee camp, past the airport, we came to a roadblock about ten feet above which there was a four-foot-high circle of sandbags sporting a nasty-looking machine gun. Down on the road, two youngish soldiers in ill-fitting uniforms and carrying automatic weapons stopped our taxi and had us roll down the windows. Without being asked, my two fellow passengers whipped out their student ID cards. Nothing wrong with this, except I hadn't brought mine. The soldier on my side of the car said something in a demanding voice to me. I answered in my best Arabic: "I don't understand." Big mistake! He pointed his weapon through the open window at my chest and screamed the request again. Miss X, who was sitting next to me, was quick to suggest that I get out and that they would send the taxi back for me. You'll have to imagine my response, because I certainly can't remember what I said in my panicky state, except that it was in rapid-fire English with a sprinkling of trailer park words. There was no way I was getting out of that taxi. The man with the gun obviously enjoyed my response and, realizing I was no terrorist, he waved us on.

When we arrived back at ACS, I was in trouble (at least officially) for the only time that year. Abraham, Dad's 1956 Crusader trip driver, was the only person who had permission to take me off campus. Considering what I'd been through, this transgression seemed trifling; in retrospect, Dad's caution made some sense.

You can bet that I was careful to bring my student ID card when ACS organized a four-day student trip (which Dad had allowed) that spring to Jerusalem and Petra. Walking the three-quarter-mile darkened gorge, with its 10-foot width and 50-foot-high walls, and then turning a corner to suddenly see Petra's treasury bathed in light, was—along with Krak des Chevaliers—the most memorable of my Middle East sightseeing moments (the movie *Indiana Jones and the Last Crusade* barely does it justice.) By the way, I was never asked to show my student ID again.

16

RANDOLPH MERIWETHER VAUGHAN

My roommate for most of my year at ACS was Randy Vaughan, perhaps the smartest person I've ever known. We met when I was not quite fifteen years old; he was ten months older. While I'd had plenty of self-reliant travels and solo experiences, ACS was my first extended time away from family. Randy became a lifelong friend, sharing with me a succession of activities that left us permanently bonded. Someday, I just might write about the ebb and flow of our meetings over the subsequent sixty years and provide some of his life highlights that occurred without my participation. Both then and since, Randy has attracted action.

Randy was born in late 1945 in New York City. At age five, his parents divorced, and he spent the next years traveling with his mom and attending various schools, domestic and foreign. The year 1959 found him in Beirut as his mother, who was from a well-to-do Pittsburgh family, had a good friend living there. That friend's Aramco-employed husband commuted back to Beirut on weekends, taking advantage of those frequent Aramco flights. After two years as a day student, where his friends included the son of a CIA agent, he became a boarder like myself at ACS. (The Beirut CIA Station Chief's son, Stewart Copeland, was also a young ACS student at this time. Music fans will recognize him as the drummer for the band the Police.)

Randy was not my first roommate—that student dumped me after a week, when it became evident that I was, in his words, "socially inept" and not prepared to focus significant time and energy pursuing girls. (That roommate was expelled later that same academic year for violating the school's alcohol policy. His was not an isolated expulsion; at least ten other classmates left that year for various offences, some far more embarrassing than drinking.) As Randy unpacked, two possessions caught my eye: a quality shortwave radio and a roulette wheel. The radio picked up the BBC station in Nicosia, Cyprus. We listened to the news and assorted programming, and for the first time in my life, I heard popular music, top forty hits from around the world. We would plot out the best program times and use his tape deck to record our favorites.

The roulette wheel, while certainly not parent approved, was to be the most educational and wealth-building aspect of my Beirut year. Our boys' dorm had about sixty residents, none of whom had enough to do, particularly on the weekends. The fact that the sons of oil workers predominated made for something of an unpleasant "Lord of the Flies" environment, typical of boarding schools. ACS also attracted the children of both well-to-do locals seeking Western educations and higher-class expats: government officials and foreign-posted businessmen. These children were mostly day students. I suspect that Randy and I were a unique roommate pair, both eventually earning status MBAs—his from Columbia, mine from Harvard. (Peter Dekom, another boarder at the time, clearly topped us all on the career success scale, however. As an attorney to Hollywood royalty, his clients have included George Lucas, John Travolta, and Ron Howard.) Typically, boarding students collected an allowance before each weekend, courtesy of their parents. Dad had neglected this. Is it any wonder that roulette became my penury solution?

After a false start with Randy "running the wheel," I took over and established odds based upon 30 rather than 36 numbers. (Our standard wheel was numbered zero to 36, with zero being a clean board sweep for the operator, or house.) So, if a player bet on 21 and that number came up, I'd pay 30 times his bet, not 36 times. Bet two numbers and win, and I'd pay 15 times, not 18. You get the picture. The exception to "Howard's odds" was a two-to-one bet on red or black, the wheel's two colors. These odds favored the house, me, and were obviously unfair, but playing was the only exciting thing for my fellow dormmates to do. The "business" thrived. What started slowly with a Saturday afternoon game gradually lasted into the wee hours of Sunday. Then popular demand led to a Friday afternoon start and two sleepless nights a weekend. An even larger game was established soon after when I successfully picked the lock of a large unused room down the hall that was meant for a resident teacher. Cigarette smoking was allowed, and we had pin-ups for decoration—it was the dorm's weekend place to be. More players, more bets, more hours, and *more money* for yours truly.

Although I remained generally frugal, my lifestyle gradually began to change; Randy and I could go on joint outings. A hotel pool that charged an entrance fee was feasible, as was eating at a restaurant. My biggest expense was buying books. Financial history had caught my fancy in addition to my earlier enthusiasm for military and ancient history. Volumes describing the campaigns of Vanderbilt, Gould, Hannibal, and Alexander were acquired from Khayat's.* Through all this, Randy never asked for a share of the profits, despite providing the wheel and the idea. All this was too good to last—and it didn't. Plus, there were negatives.

Aramco flew its Beirut students back to Arabia for spring vacation in 1962. By then I had more money than I knew what to do with. I asked Dad to help me set up an interest-earning savings account in the States. This he was more than willing to do, no questions asked. But Dad was no dummy when it came to the behavior of young men. In the days that followed my return from spring break, unseen forces entered the Randy-Richard world. First, the headmaster unexpectedly called me into his office and casually asked how I was doing. Next, a late Saturday night session was interrupted, the bets confiscated, and our gambling den securely locked. Roulette became a banned activity. Finally came the cruelest blow

---

* Hart, Dodge, and Josephson were my favorite authors, and at age fifteen I rooted for the underdogs, not the Romans or the robber barons.

of all: Randy, the "bad influence," was moved to another room with a different roommate less than a month before the school year ended. To this day, he stridently and reasonably maintains that he was the innocent party and was unfairly punished. Point taken.

Chief among the other negatives of my gambling enterprise was that I accumulated few other ACS friends. Life is a cooperative endeavor, and friends had and have always helped me, as I have helped them. Roulette players aren't likely to feel kindly toward someone who takes their money. Serious, committed students did not perceive me as a kindred spirit, and I didn't have the free time to spend with them. Teachers are not blind; they saw how tired I was on Mondays and were not impressed with my extracurricular activities. By any reasonable standard I should have gotten an A grade in my ancient history class; instead I got a B-minus. My other grades were much worse, deservedly so, although the D-minus received in French I was a gift. (If spelling English words was a problem for me, imagine the challenge presented by French ones.) I had acquired a sort of anti-halo and was smart enough to vow that it would not happen in the future. What I didn't understand was how hard it was and how long it would take to turn that around.

Of the many adventures Randy and I shared that year in Beirut, the most memorable featured a tarantula. Let me set the scene: The night had been hot and muggy, and I was bare-chested, wearing only underwear briefs and lying under a thin bed sheet. Dawn had broken and, upon waking, I noticed a strange tickling on my lower leg. A brown, hairy tarantula larger than my hand was advancing steadily along my sheet-covered leg toward my knee. Fifteen-year-old males are typically concerned with their manly demeanor. Not me. I screamed like a little girl, waking Randy and most of the dorm. In one motion I shot from a supine position to standing on my desk. Only a fictional superhero could have moved as fast. Randy, bless his heart, took in the situation instantly. He grabbed a metal-edged eighteen-inch wooden ruler off his desk and turned to confront the intruder. Recognizing the unequal combat ahead, the tarantula hightailed it out under our door. As Randy pursued it, I quaked on my desk. Down the hall they raced, the spider looking for an escape route. He turned into another doorway but could not squeeze under the door—his first mistake. His second was to keep trying, running back and forth in the thirty-six-inch space while Randy rained down deadly-but-poorly-aimed ruler blows. Finally, one leg was amputated, then another. Now he was an easier target, and the end came quickly. I arrived to see twenty or so hairy tarantula parts, many still wiggling.

Our last days in Beirut were anticlimactic. We still spent time together, but there was no more roulette, and while ACS was willing to let us enter the eleventh grade, our families had other plans. On the strength of my strong secondary school admissions test scores and the likely pull Dad had through his non-Aramco activities (more on that in chapter 21), I would be going back to the States, to Cranbrook School outside of Detroit, Michigan. Randy was headed to the very similar Shady Side Academy outside of Pittsburgh, where his grandparents, the Todds, had some clout. Both schools were in fact in the same athletic conference, and I would compete at Shady Side on several occasions in the years ahead, always renewing contact with Randy. We would both be repeating the tenth grade, although Randy—incredibly—was later able to skip eleventh. Before that, however, Randy would come and visit me for three weeks in Ras Tanura over the summer, where he hoped to romance Jan, the girl you met a few pages back. We expected our paths would then diverge; in that we were happily mistaken.

Leaving ACS was absolutely the right thing to do. No matter how much effort I might have expended, I would never have escaped from the anti-halo acquired that first year. It was hard enough at Cranbrook, as I was about to find out.

GOLDEN SPECULATION

In the summer of 1962, I started turning savings into wealth. That journey began where my Bratdom began … Al Khobar. With the approximately $50 that I had kept in hand from my roulette "earnings," I wanted to buy a gold coin. (A higher standard of living and my new 3-percent-earning savings account had absorbed the rest. Babysitting other peoples' children was now my major source of income.) I headed back to Khobar and to the money changers I'd visited so frequently in years past. Back then, I would pick up the odd piece of change from all over the world, never paying even the face value. Not that face value was relevant; remember that Dutch ten-guilder note? Now I was looking for bigger game.

My first purchase of a small Turkish gold coin for about US $6 wasn't very satisfying. While buying it, however, I saw the money changer had US ten- and twenty-dollar gold pieces, better known as eagles and double eagles, respectively. I had a penny collection, and I knew that some dates were more valuable than others. I also knew that a coin in good condition could be worth considerably more than one in poor condition. Back in Ras Tanura, I headed straight to the library and examined a book on coin collecting. Yes, there were gold coin dates that were worth more, some much more. I carefully wrote them down, and the following week I headed back to my Khobar money changers. Not surprisingly, none of the premium dates were for sale. But there were many shades of quality available, and in Khobar all $10 eagles sold for the equivalent of $18.75, give or take a nickel.

After considering the coins at various shops, I bought an eagle dated in the 1880s. While not "uncirculated," the highest classification, it would probably grade "very fine," the second highest (and, I told myself, certainly no worse than "fine"). The next step in my plan was to get it to the United States, not quite as easy as it sounds. Yes, I was flying there at summer's end, but at that time, U.S. citizens were not allowed to import gold into the country. Owning gold was also against the law, period, but legitimate coin collections—consisting of coins minted before 1933—were allowed. Another risk also bothered me: What if I lost the coin?

I had watched enough customs inspectors over the years to know exactly the focus of their distrust for teenage boys: drug smuggling. Wear sloppy clothes, have long, unkempt dirty hair, and you were asking to have your luggage, and possibly your body, strip searched. Follow the Boy Scout laws and oath, and the worse that would happen is that one piece of your luggage, probably your carry-on, might be inspected. (Apparently the incongruity of my action plan in the context of my high

Boy Scout rank escaped me. You can't, however, say I ignored the Scout motto: Be prepared.) With my short blond hair and skinny frame clad in clean clothes, I had half the battle won. To supplement this preparation, I carefully placed the eagle in a small paper coin envelope and pinned the envelope, and therefore the coin, in the bottom of my front right trouser pocket. Genius. I could feel the coin to reassure myself that it was there without drawing attention. To lose the coin or have it stolen would require losing my pants. The journey to America went off without a hitch. Within the first month I went to the J. L. Hudson department store in downtown Detroit. The manager of the coin department took one look at my eagle and offered me $25, which I accepted on the spot. I had a 33.3 percent return in four months—this was way better than a savings account. Today, these transactions might sound small, but if you multiply it by fifty to account for the change in the price of gold, you get a better idea of their context in my life.

The following summer, 1963, I bought four high-quality eagles, followed the same transportation mechanics, and sold them at Hudson's for $25 apiece. But I didn't like the way the manager looked at me when he handed over the cash. My days of bargaining had taught me a lot. The next summer I planned to buy six coins and sell four in Pittsburgh and two in Detroit. Things worked out much better.

My first trip to Khobar, that summer of 1964, I bought two eagles of "very fine" quality from a money changer who quickly understood, despite no indication from me, that I was looking for quality.* After money and coins changed hands, he motioned that he wanted to show me something else. He brought forth a gold coin about the size and weight of a $20 gold piece. It had an undersized American eagle on one side and descriptive information—weight and gold percentage—on the other. This was a dealer who had never exhibited a counterfeit King

Minted in 1945 and 1946, these coins were used to pay Aramco's royalty to the Saudi Arabian government. As such, they are unique: part American, part Saudi, and 100 percent Aramco. I paid $39 for mine and sold it in Pittsburgh two months later for $80. Upon reading my letter recounting the success, Dad bought six of the coins. Today these coins, in poor condition, sell for about $4,000. I always paid a tiny bit extra to buy coins in the best possible condition.

---

* I was continually amazed by how quickly the money changers were able to deduce my inner thoughts no matter how hard I tried to disguise them. I consider this recognition to be one of the most valuable professional investing lessons stemming from my youth: be aware of other people's ability to understand you and their motivations in your transactions.

George V sovereign, and the price ($39) was right.* Had it been $5 or an even worse $10 lower, I would have walked away because, if genuine, the gold alone was worth near $35. Despite my uncertainty, I bought it and, my funds almost exhausted, headed back to Ras Tanura.

The RT library boosted my knowledge of that coin considerably. They were minted in Philadelphia between 1945 and 1946 to pay Aramco's royalty due the Saudi government. Called Saudi 4 Pounds, they were considered a rarity, but due to their date post-1933 were not particularly sought after by collectors. At least that's what the book said. Well, maybe they *were* sought after. I sold mine for $80 to the Gimbels department store coin manager in Pittsburgh. He also paid me $25 each for the four $10 eagles I had also acquired that summer. Total capital committed: $114. Revenue generated: $180. Profit: $66 or a 57 percent return. In my three summers of gold speculation, I had netted profits about equal to the money I'd acquired in my entire ACS roulette activities. This was way more fun and intellectually challenging: no missing sleep, no breathing cigarette smoke, no "customer" cheating. Avaricious visions brightened my future.

Leading up to my summer vacation in 1965, this 18-year-old carefully planned his coin transaction and

---

* An enterprising con man had taken advantage of the Turkish exit from Arabia during World War I and passed a goodly number of counterfeit English sovereigns. Money changers would never try to sell you these; they'd be risking losing a hand (rough justice, indeed). If, however, you were stupid enough to pick one out of their display and want it ...

transportation strategy. In Khobar I would buy six eagles, which would be sold to retail customers, one teacher and five students at Cranbrook, who had responded to my small note posted on the dorm bulletin board. I would also bring back two of the high-margin Saudi 4 Pounds to sell one at a time to high-end coin shops. My capital at risk would be $190, my revenue $310, and expected profit $120. It was a sound plan: nothing to invite the suspicion of customs agents. Only cash transactions, no paper trail to follow from the coin shop buyers back to my travel. I had a hollow metal deodorant can for the eagles and would pin the 4 Pounds into my left and right front pockets. Like many plans, however sound, it did not survive events. My family was lost in the Cairo crash, and I did not return to Arabia for ten long years, by which time the price of gold had tripled and much of the profit opportunity had disappeared. Furthermore, I was no longer a kid. While the chance of being arrested remained minimal, the profit-consequences ratio wasn't worth the risk.

There's one addendum to my youthful gold speculation adventure. When friends in Ras Tanura went through the many possessions my family left behind after the Cairo crash, they found Dad owned six of the Saudi 4 Pounds coins. He had obviously purchased them after receiving my letter recounting my activities. Despite my plea that these coins somehow be sent on to me, they were sold along with the VW Microbus we were scheduled to pick up later in Germany. Those two sales, plus selling the many other Howard household effects in Arabia, generated a total of nearly $10,000, an amount that more than paid for my college and graduate school tuition (for a general sense of what this amount is worth in today's dollars, multiply by ten, or at least that's what government statistics suggest). Mom's Irish harp was saved, and I still have it. As the years have passed, knowing that Dad had chosen to bet his money on my judgment and skill is more valuable to me than any possible profit those coins may have brought.

CRANBROOK SCHOOL

In late August 1962, Mom and I headed to the United States and Cranbrook School in Bloomfield Hills, Michigan. At the time, I found it strange that the year before I could fly alone to Beirut, while now, going to Detroit, I needed Mom's accompaniment. She was, however, quite helpful: buying me some clothes, getting me enrolled at Cranbrook, lining up an orthodontist for my horrible teeth, and starting me as a patient at Henry Ford Hospital (recurring diarrhea being an unwelcome souvenir from my time in Beirut). My three solo Saturday trips to that hospital involved walking about two miles along Lone Pine Road, which fronted the Cranbrook campus, to its intersection with Woodward Avenue. At this main four-lane thoroughfare into the center of Detroit, I would catch a direct bus to the hospital; it also gave me easy access to the J.L. Hudson coin department. Both getting to the hospital and coming back took more than an hour, and I had to build in a margin of safety. What they did to me at Henry Ford is not fit for polite conversation, but admittedly the kidney stones I had years later were a worse experience. Trips to the orthodontist involved similar steps, although I often skipped the shorter bus ride and walked the whole way. Occasionally a day student, passing by with a car, would pick me up and save me the walk.

Although there were plenty of similarities, Cranbrook was nothing like ACS. The food was better, the teachers were better, the dorm rooms were better (all were singles), and the grounds were spectacular. The Cranbrook community included an elementary school, a science museum, an art academy, an Episcopal church, and both a girls' school and a boys' school for grades seven through twelve. The students were typically very well off, mostly from Detroit's wealthy or executive-class families. Next to me in European history class, for example, sat Mitt

I spent three years at Cranbrook School in Bloomfield Hills, Michigan: making the grades, meeting Yvette, and scoring high on the SATs. Dad took this picture when we visited in 1961. While Mom and Beth posed, the headmaster was showing me the athletic facilities. I recognized Joe Schmidt, an NFL Hall of Fame linebacker, walking out as we were walking in (the Lions were using Cranbrook for their preseason training).

Romney, son of the American Motors Corporation president (many years later he ran for president of the United States; he would have been a good one). There were a few faculty children and scholarship recipients, but even this group was better off financially than I perceived myself to be. Aramco footed my primary bill: room and board and tuition, but there were other daunting expenses to maneuver. My gym clothes, for example, came at ten cents an item from the unclaimed lost and found. On an eight-day track team trip I survived on bread, cucumbers, and peanut butter when meals were not provided. My teammates ate at restaurants.

The students there were plenty smart, and some, particularly the day students, were obviously getting parental help with their studies. It was going to be a challenge competing with this group academically, and things didn't look hopeful my first year. I immediately dropped certain trailer park and oil camp words from my vocabulary in order to fit in—learning to knot a tie and wear a sportscoat (both required) was easy in comparison. I did fine in math class, but in English class and European history my papers and tests, despite containing what I perceived as significant insights, were constantly being marked down for spelling mistakes.

The teachers knew I was repeating tenth grade and treated me accordingly, expecting my work to be substandard and grading it thus. Most of my weekends were entirely devoted to writing assignments, endlessly trying to get words spelled properly before struggling to type the papers. Erasable typing paper and gobs of liquid Wite-Out were essential. I once spent four hours with a dictionary trying to spell "obvious" correctly before giving up and rewriting the sentence using another word. As for the French I class I was forced to repeat, moving from Lebanon to Michigan didn't change my language aptitude.*

The best thing that happened my first year at Cranbrook, and indeed in my entire life, occurred thanks to my transportation struggles. The Wednesday before Thanksgiving, classes let out at noon and I was headed to Sturgis, Michigan, and to my mother's younger sister's family, the Belands, for vacation. It was the usual walk and bus ride into the center of Detroit, where I caught a Greyhound bus headed toward Chicago with countless intermediate stops. It was dark and cold when I got to the little town of Marshall about halfway across the state. There I used a pay phone to call my aunt, who was expecting my call, and an hour later she picked me up and drove me home, altogether about an eight-hour trip. After three days in family warmth, I spent all of Sunday reversing the journey.

When Christmas vacation neared, the dorm's resident teacher said that I should call Mrs. Daunic, a math

---

* My revenge was a long time coming. As a university trustee 40 years later, my assigned committee heard a long presentation on importance of foreign culture and why our school should consider requiring foreign language courses. Initially, I restrained myself during the considerable discussion. Finally, however, I weighed in and opined that computers were sure to achieve instant foreign language translation soon, and that auto mechanics seemed like a better use of our students' time. The room fell very silent.... As I explained before, you can't get the trailer park completely out of the boy.

teacher at Cranbrook's girls' school (which was called Kingswood) across the lake. She would be going to visit her family in Sturgis and might possibly take me along. I called, and indeed she would give me a ride. And what a trip it turned out to be. Sitting next to me in the front seat was her daughter, Yvette, a sophomore at Kingswood. This was about the prettiest girl I had ever seen, and she had other noticeable attributes including obvious smarts. Of course, since I was socially inept, it took almost a year for this relationship to get started, but eventually it did. After a second ride to Sturgis the following Thanksgiving, I finally got up sufficient courage to ask her out on a movie date.

By then I was a junior and, although firmly positioned near the bottom of my class academically, I was beginning to make progress. My English teacher, God love him, was into literary quotations. These I found interesting, and in this spelling wasn't much of an issue. Yvette, one of her class's top students, was proofing my weekend papers, which improved and speeded them along dramatically. I was taking French I for the third time and—while I'd end up getting a D-plus, despite the teacher's valiant efforts—it no longer absorbed huge amounts of frustrating time. American history was enjoyable and math class not impossible. I had friends who (based upon my grades) thought me a slacker, but not completely stupid. I had a girlfriend; life was good. How the teachers thought of me was revealed one day in late spring when, walking toward my dorm across the beautiful Cranbrook grounds after a Saturday date, I saw a married couple coming in the opposite direction. The husband taught Latin, the wife

English—one at each school. Seeing me they stopped and spoke to each other. As I neared, the husband asked in a querulous tone, "Are you dating Yvette Daunic?" When I answered politely in the affirmative, he turned to his wife and said, "There's no explaining these things." At the time, I inwardly seethed but quickly came to regard the comment as a compliment. Who deserved the best girlfriend? Me!

It was about this time that I first took the standardized tests (SATs) then required of all high school students seeking college entry. Suddenly, I had four huge advantages: First, and most important, since everything was multiple choice, my flawed spelling didn't matter. Second, parental help no longer directly influenced results, although I suppose some of my fellow students may have had prep

It took a while, but eventually I got the best girlfriend. Who could possibly be more deserving?

courses. Third, and most unusual, was the experience I'd had years before taking similar tests in elementary school, when I couldn't read. How did that help? Back then, I had learned to focus my attention on the answer choices. Similar words in two answers almost invariably meant that one of them was right and that one contained a common error. Make an educated guess between the two and you're going to do a lot better than a student who focuses on the question and, not knowing the answer, guesses randomly. Fourth, my athletics, although only marginally successful, had hardened me to competition stress. I could (and would) consume endless Canada Mints and easily work feverishly for three hours on a sugar high.

Six months and three sets of tests later, I was finally near the top of my Cranbrook class in something non athletic. I'd scored a 1400 combined on the key math and verbal tests, and also had three 700-plus scores on achievement tests. When our student newspaper printed my name among our class's top five test scorers, there was disbelief and raised eyebrows. I like to think my hard work at Cranbrook paid off, but sadly, my teachers' and friends' perceptions were slow to change. (For example, I was excluded from a senior year Eastern European extracurricular study activity reserved for the "better" students, despite my impending 1965 summer trip through Yugoslavia.) But it was not a fluke. When I took a similar graduate business school test four years later, I again scored in the top one percent nationally. I suspect those results, along with being my university's student senate president, played a significant role in my Harvard Business School acceptance.

SUMMER OF '64

Dad may have never helped me with my schoolwork, but you can't say he didn't give me educational experiences. Case in point: After finishing up eleventh grade, I flew to London for an overnight, and the following evening landed in Tehran, Iran. The taxi ride to the hotel soon got exciting; the Shah landed about 60 minutes after I did. He, of course, didn't have to clear customs or wait for his luggage and was right behind me on the drive into the city. Surging, screaming mobs, some shouting "death to the Shah" while others cheered him on, couldn't have cared less about me, but they were frightening regardless. My driver eventually got us onto a side street, where he spent his time keeping demonstrators from standing on his hood. I slunk down in the back seat trying very hard not to attract attention.

When I eventually got to the hotel, I found that Mom and Dad were delayed and would not arrive until the next day (Beth had been left in Arabia). Tehran had some spectacular buildings and avenues, but in other respects it was a typical Middle Eastern city, its drivers the worst I had ever seen. Thankfully, three days later we were all in Isfahan, the medieval capital. As usual, my body clock had trouble recalibrating, and I was up every morning before dawn and walking around that beautiful city before joining my parents for an early lunch and afternoon sightseeing. On one walk, I came upon a small artist's studio and was drawn to a painting of a three-camel caravan in the window. The proprietor saw my interest, came out, explained that he was Sumbat, the artist, and invited me in for tea. I declined his invitation but noted the location so that I could stop by the next day with my parents.

Our family had never purchased any original artwork, and we weren't about to start with a $250 painting, no matter how magnificent. But Mom, ever the artist, dabbled in painting, and Dad had an idea. Would the artist visit the Aramco compounds and give lessons? Perhaps. My parents did buy six much less expensive works, and early the following year, Sumbat Der Kiureghian was in Ras Tanura and then Dhahran giving painting lessons.* When he left the Aramco communities after about six weeks, the artist gave my parents the caravan painting as a thank-you. I still have that painting, along with other

---

* Forty-five years later, Sumbat's son Armen published *The Life and Art of Sumbat*. In the book he graciously credits my parents for his dad's financially and artistically successful Aramco interlude. Serendipitously, Armen, a UC Berkeley engineering professor and earthquake authority, noted my last name when I ordered that book. Curious, he tracked me down. We became fast friends, visiting each other in Connecticut, San Francisco, and New York City. Thanks to him I have acquired additional paintings.

Thanks to my early morning wanderings in Isfahan, Mom and Dad were introduced to Sumbat Der Kiureghian, an Iranian artist of Armenian heritage. In March 1965 he stayed with my parents while giving painting lessons to Aramcons. While there he painted this dhow picture (top), which I purchased many years later. When leaving Ras Tanura, he gifted the picture of the camel caravan to my parents as a thank-you. Both now hang in my dining room.

"Sumbats" I've acquired over the years. Just as important, a new element of culture entered my personal world.

After one week in Iran, we headed back to Arabia, where my summer moved at a brisk pace. Dad was working a shift as temporary Home Ownership department head in Dhahran, sleeping there five nights a week at Steineke Hall. The plan was that when the incumbent returned from vacation, Dad would leave the department, move back to RT, and begin a new job in the refinery. He'd be leaving behind a legacy of more than 600 homes for Saudi employees and the community he'd lavished with attention—Rahimah.

Most Wednesdays I would take a morning bus to Dhahran and continue on to Khobar, where I'd hunt gold coins. Truth be told, I just loved walking around my old haunts, buying bread and talking with shop-keepers and money changers. By the time Dad got out of work on those Wednesdays, I would have gotten back to Dhahran, and we'd have dinner together and talk about his job, my potential college education, and the world generally. The refinery was a major topic, more specifically, why wasn't it profitable? Dad thought that since every refinery investment had a three-year-or-less payback, it wasn't logical that the whole thing lost money. A dozen years later I could explain why, as well as the subtle and not so subtle intricacies of refinery economics. At that time, however, it was a mystery to both of us. We'd play Ping-Pong and pool, activities where I'd take a little off my game, worried that my father, the ultimate competitor, would get discouraged if he kept losing. In shuffleboard we were closely matched. After spending the night with Dad in his room, Thursday mornings I'd read at Steineke Hall or the Dhahran library until Dad was done at noon. Then we'd head to Ras Tanura and be home about an hour later. On one of those rides, Dad confided in me that he intended to work for Aramco until he retired. The normal retirement age was 60, but hopefully he'd move into top management and get an extra five years.

Three or four Friday mornings that summer, Dad had me out near the water wells that served Ras Tanura. I was getting driving lessons. It was essential that I learn to drive a standard transmission vehicle, and this deserted area had upgrades where shifting into higher or lower gears was a suitable challenge. So why was I doing this? In case of emergencies, I was told; then came the shock of shocks. Next summer, after my graduation, we would be heading to Germany, picking up a VW Microbus, and driving it back to Arabia. I pointed out the obvious flaws in this plan: We'd be going behind the Iron Curtain and crossing some less-than-civilized stretches of Turkey and Syria—2,500 miles of driving even before we got to Arabia. Then 750 miles along the pipeline in the middle of summer. Plus, why did our family need an eight-passenger bus? The curt answer was that Dad was part of a group of ex-naval officers that were responsible for keeping the refinery out of Russian hands. They might well need the bus, and crossing Yugoslavia wouldn't be a problem. Okay. I knew when to stop questioning.

With about three weeks to go before I was to head back to America, Dad dropped an even bigger Friday morning surprise. I needed practice shooting a revolver. (Up to that point I had never once heard him speak about having a gun or shooting one.) Out we went into the desert with a 24-by-24-inch plywood target and three different pistols, one a Luger. My takeaway from that experience: don't believe what you see in the movies. It is very hard to hit a chest-size object from even ten feet, and near impossible at thirty. The Luger, by the way, had a kick and I learned you'd better be braced when firing. I did most of the shooting, but when Dad did a little, it was obvious he was good. When we finished, there was no doubt that I couldn't be counted on to hit anything and that the lightest weapon was the right one for me. In hindsight this was pretty close to a proverbial "smoking gun," but the obvious still hadn't seeped into my consciousness. Forty-five years later it finally did . . . and it is all spelled out in chapter 21.

Considering my many unusual experiences in the summer of 1964, most would probably be surprised at what seemed most unusual to me at the time. It was courtesy of my sister, Beth. One afternoon I was reading in my room with the door open when she came home from school with two of her third-grade girlfriends. Not knowing I could hear them, they were discussing boys, specifically the boys they were going to marry. I was nine years older, in love for the first time, and marriage had never occurred to me. (Four years later, I would be walking down the aisle with Yvette.) As for poor Mark, John, and Yanni, whoever and wherever you are today, you three had targets on your backs. Other more consistent activities of that summer were enduring a teacher friend of Mom's spelling lessons once a week, playing basketball, and going on dawn runs in preparation for the fall cross-country season. By the way, even at dawn it was brutally hot, and Ras Tanura's location usually meant 100 percent humidity at that time of day.

Early that summer, I had sent requests for course catalogs from about a dozen colleges that looked to be possible fits. The schools were both those Cranbrook had recommended and also a half-dozen small midwestern ones that had some engineering. As these arrived by mail, I studied them closely. I was not going to any school where there was a foreign language requirement. Cranbrook's recommendations were, quite frankly, ridiculous. For example, how was I going to get to schools that weren't on major bus routes? I also had to be near an international airport, plus there was the little issue of cost. Dad had always maintained that I would have to pay my own way, but at this point he did soften a bit. He would pay for my freshman year, and if I got all A's, he might continue to pay a portion of the next three years of expenses. (Dad hadn't gotten college-related financial help from his parents. Plus, he had been a high school valedictorian and never could grasp the notion that being the top Cranbrook student might be challenging for me.) Just another reason to avoid taking any foreign language courses.

At the end of the summer, armed with a Rand McNally map of Ohio, Indiana, and Illinois—plus a few pages torn from five school catalogs—I headed back to the States. After a short rest with friends in Pittsburgh (where I also sold my gold coins), I arrived unannounced at what I thought was my first choice. Ohio Northern University's admissions office was not terribly helpful. No one was available to see me, even though I could see the head of

The Howard family, together one last time. We are outside the then-new Dhahran airport. Within the hour, I will be boarding a Pan Am flight to London, with intermediate stops. After an overnight stay I'll fly first to Boston and then to Pittsburgh, where I'll begin my college-hunting tour. Five gold coins are carefully hidden on my body (airport metal detectors are years in the future).

admissions sitting at his desk doing paperwork. Could I see the freshman dorms? "No, the dorms are locked." Was there a student who I could talk to about the school, who could maybe show me around? "Sure, just ask anyone you see out there in the hall." After eating lunch with an uniformed girl who volunteered as my guide, I picked up my suitcase, walked to the town's bus station, and continued my journey—pretty sure I wasn't going to enroll at that school. I was frugal and did not have particularly high standards; all of my hotels were dumps near bus stops, the most expensive one charging just $5 a night.

The script was pretty much repeated at two of the other four schools I visited. At the other two, an admissions staffer did talk to me, and at one of those, Millikin University, I actually got to see a dorm room. Millikin, which had looked like my second choice back in Arabia, also had two other checks in the plus column: First, the staffer, James Kettelkamp, took me home to his house for a soup lunch. Second, he drove me back to the bus station, saving me a long walk. Upon such small occurrences big decisions are made, and Millikin eventually became my school of choice.

When the fifth visit ended, I was near Chicago and able to get a bus headed back to Detroit. From that downtown station, I hopped my usual Woodward bus and knocked on Yvette's door on Lone Pine Road long after dark, exhausted. Mrs. Daunic drove me the two miles to Cranbrook and the start of my senior year the next morning.

In hindsight, it's obvious that I should have done a lot of things differently on my college-hunting trip. Arriving alone and on foot did not impress people with my ability to pay. In most cases, I could have at least phoned the day before to let them know I was coming. But how many seventeen-year-olds without parental guidance would have done as well? Or had the courage to just keep going? Three years later, when I had decided to apply to Harvard Business School (HBS), I did call and let them know I was coming for a visit. The HBS admissions staffer and I carried on a polite, far-ranging, hour long conversation, which ended when he told me there was little chance I'd be accepted. With steam coming out of my ears, this Aramco Brat left saying, "We'll see about that." I was also accepted to the Northwestern MBA program.

20

AFTER THE CRASH

While Dad was breathing his last and mourning Mom and Beth in the early hours of May 20, here in Michigan it was the evening of May 19. We were required to attend a dorm-room study hall from 7:30 to 9:30 p.m. There was, however, a five-minute break at 8:30, after which there was little chance of my absence being noted. That night, after hearing "Mr. Tambourine Man" on the radio for the first time, I climbed out of my ground-floor window, stayed in the shadows of the Cranbrook buildings, and walked just beyond the Cranbrook campus to a phone booth and called Yvette. As usual, she and I talked for nearly an hour before I casually slipped in among my fellow boarders as they milled around following the conclusion of study hall. I never worried about any penalty for being caught for skipping out on study hall; my circumstances essentially always confined me to campus anyway. I did, however, worry about upsetting my dorm's resident teacher, who always looked so pained whenever I missed chapel in order to finish an assignment, my typical rules infraction. In fact, were he alive today this paragraph wouldn't have been written.

Senior year had gone well. Back in September, Dad had sent a letter saying in no uncertain terms that he did not want me taking French II, and amazingly Cranbrook respected his wishes. I was allowed to take chemistry instead, even though my resulting five-course selection now also included physics and was considered "too difficult" for such a poor student. Freed of a certain F and an enormous pointless time commitment, I responded by getting either A's or B-pluses in all my subjects. Millikin had seen those grades, my SAT test scores, and the application that Yvette had checked for spelling, and they granted me both admittance and a significant merit scholarship. I was pleased; Mom and Dad were ecstatic. They didn't have long to enjoy the moment.

When I awoke on the 20th, I heard about a crash in Cairo on the morning radio news, but I wasn't sure which flight my family was on. Dad's last letter spoke of leaving on the 20th not the 19th ... so I decided not to worry. Physics and chemistry were my first two classes that day, they were my favorites, and once there I became totally engaged and forgot about the news. There was a break before my third class, and I went back to my dorm room to drop off and pick up books. Not thinking, I turned on the radio again and now I heard that the PIA flight had originated in Karachi and stopped in Dhahran. Again, I decided not to worry, but headed to math class, albeit with a nagging feeling of unease.

Early in that class, Mr. Penny, one of the track coaches and my tenth-grade history teacher, came to the room with a horrible look on his face. He asked me to gather my books and leave with him; I knew right then my family was on the flight. We walked together for what seemed like forever, with him struggling to say whatever he was going to say. Finally, in the grassy area behind my dorm, he told me that my family had been lost in the crash. At first it didn't hit me very hard. I didn't know it, but subconsciously I could deal with losing Dad; our separations had prepared me. A dozen years of fighting and scheming for his attention was over. However, when Mr. Penny made it clear that Beth had also died, I dropped to the ground stunned. It is said that nothing hurts like losing your child, and for all emotional intents and purposes, Beth was my child. It hurt bad.

The next minute or two were filled with poor Mr. Penny spouting platitudes. For a man who'd thrown chalk at me thirty months before (for obnoxiously flaunting my knowledge of the battle of Jutland in European history class), this wasn't shaping up to be a good day for him either. His discomfort eased my own; I got up and said I'd better drop off my math book in my dorm room and get to English class. Thankfully, the school had thought this through, and he told me no, I was done for the week. They'd been in contact with my Aunt Betsy in Sturgis; Mr. Penny would drive me there.

That afternoon and the next day in Sturgis, I dealt with four telephone calls: An abrupt, New York-based Aramco employee whose tone said he didn't even pretend to care about my situation. Two pushy newspaper reporters. Best, our old friend and neighbor from Khobar days, Victor Vella. It had been eight years since we'd spoken, and I was touched that he'd tracked me down based solely on the newspaper reports. Vic was heartbroken and said all the right things, but he wanted me to organize a memorial service. I just couldn't do it. The logistics were beyond me and the question of where we would hold it was daunting. There *was* a memorial in Arabia, but no one thought to include me, and Vic, long separated from Aramco, couldn't get a visa. I wish they had flown me back; if so, my grieving might have started and gotten over decades sooner.

That Thursday night, the *Huntley-Brinkley Report* on NBC featured coverage of the crash. Thankfully, I didn't watch (but Yvette did, and remembering it even fifty-six years later brought her to tears).* The next morning, Friday, I was up at five a.m. and walked to the Sturgis newsstand. The *New York Times* and two other papers headlined the crash with graphic body-part pictures. One was of a Caucasian woman's leg; it had to be my mother's, the only white woman on the plane.

After class Friday, Mrs. Daunic and Yvette drove to Sturgis. At the time, I was profoundly grateful, and with the passing of years that feeling has strengthened. Yvette and her mom really got my life back on track over those next two days. On Sunday, we three drove back to school. The next few weeks to graduation were tough. Most students and the teachers, in particular, found it hard to look

---

* Peter and William Love, sons of Donald, have carried the same scar and also tear up when talking about the crash and their watching of the *Huntley-Brinkley Report*. Writing this memoir has led to the Howards and Loves finding each other. We hope to gather or at least call each other every anniversary of the crash going forward. On May 22, 2021, we did just that.

at me. Everyone knew of my tragedy; it was international news and the way to give it local interest in the Michigan newspapers was to reference me. There was no place to hide. After a haircut, I started back to the barbershop realizing I hadn't left a tip. The barber and three men I didn't know were talking quietly, and I heard one say, "What can you possibly say to that boy?" I turned on my heel and slipped away unnoticed.

I didn't know our new chaplain and didn't want to confide in him, so I just bottled up my feelings and went on, determined to succeed. Mostly I did fine, thanks to four of my dorm friends and Yvette. At our athletic league's year-end track meet, I should have won the half-mile run, but I just couldn't get focused, knowing that Dad had said he'd be there to watch. He had never seen me run and had seen only one of my many basketball games. I finished fifth in the race, the same as the year before. The idea that graduation meant separation from all my Cranbrook friends tormented me. At the ceremony, I sobbed uncontrollably. The tears just wouldn't stop while I walked in the procession. I vowed that hereafter I would never let anyone know about the crash. (That often proved impossible.) What no one, except possibly another Brat, could understand is that I hadn't just lost my family; I'd also lost all my RT friends, my parents' friends, and the Ras Tanura community I loved.

The fifty-six years that have followed have been good years. My uncle, Melvin Beland, really stepped up as my guardian, driving me to Millikin, helping me get summer jobs, and, importantly, provided business management exposure. He treated me like a son and from the very beginning showed an expectation that I would be successful in college and life. At Millikin I earned a welding engineering degree, fulfilling my dream of nine years before when visiting the Trans Arabian Pipeline, plus I got an industrial engineering degree. Two years later, at Harvard Business School, I got a finance-focused MBA. I spent the money from selling my family's belongings and the money Dad had so painfully and carefully saved for my education. Plus, I knew that an investing career would help me manage the money that would eventually come my way as a result of litigation with the airline. It was paltry in the context of later similar awards, and today it is obvious that I should have asked the Aramco Legal Department to help me in this regard. It's also obvious that rather than saying "we are here to help you," Aramco management should have made some specific suggestions instead of letting an eighteen-year-old with an unsophisticated family fend for himself. Exxon, on the other hand, sprang into action to help the Love family when their husband and father, Donald, the only other American on the flight, was lost in the crash. The comparison is jarring. Strangely, however, my struggles and mistakes worked to my benefit in the long run. At every turn I examined my actions and failures. I learned that when it comes to finance, you do not rely on the kindness of strangers—most mistakes I made only once.

After Harvard, there were four good, high-paying investment management companies to work for: CIGNA, Fidelity (where Frank Jungers, retired Aramco president, was kind enough to stop by and say he remembered Dad fondly), T. Rowe Price, and Prospector Partners, my best posting. All these firms, to a large extent, put up with my "chip on the shoulder" attitude stemming from my youthful school experiences. Talk about a contrary investor, talk about skepticism toward accepted truth—I was a natural. Happily, my work has often involved energy securities and has kept me informed of the progress of what is now Saudi Aramco. For my forty-seven-and-one-half-year career, I always saved at least 10 percent of my annual salary and sometimes much more. Plus, I've had occasional financial windfalls, à la the Saudi 4 Pounds purchase, when my knowledge and my willingness to accept risk aligned with opportunity to my satisfaction.*

Throughout those years, I've accumulated many good friends who have helped me and have taught me a lot. Perhaps the most insightful, ego-stabilizing wisdom came from a boss who preached, "You're never as good as good-performance numbers say you are and never as bad as bad numbers suggest." A succession of very competent assistants corrected my spelling, and today, word

---

* Another digression: When the Alaskan North Slope oil fields were being developed, the biggest issue for investors was the Trans Alaskan Pipeline and its welding. Two hundred securities analysts, representing financial firms from all over the world, were flown to Alaska for presentations. I was the only analyst there with a welding engineering degree. Unlike the others, who had to take things largely on faith, I could ask relevant technical questions of the men in the field who were responsible. I came away knowing the welding was sound and that the problem, never actually stated due to litigation concerns, was inspection record keeping. This was going to work, and I "bet the farm." It may well have been my "finest hour" as an investor.

processors and spellcheck have replaced Jane Hirsch and Barb Derry. At first, I was personally way too frugal, and I've always invested my employers and their clients' money perhaps too cautiously, subconsciously afraid of the reversals of fortune that dogged my early life. Today my two fantastic sons refer to me as "the new dad," seemingly willing to spend on many extravagances. Yvette has been with me ever since that ride to Sturgis and knows my flaws only too well. I owe the Aramco community big time, but I owe her most of all.

AN AGENT IN PLACE

At my fortieth Cranbrook class reunion, Greg Dearth, our track team's quarter miler asked, "Was your dad in the CIA?" "No, certainly not," was my reply. Five years later, at our forty-fifth, I was curious enough to ask Greg what had prompted his question. He had read *Who's Who in the CIA,* authored by Julius Mader, an East German journalist with Stasi connections. Included among those listed was Harry Hoey, our old headmaster. That identification, plus plenty of other circumstantial evidence, led Greg to conclude that Cranbrook had served as a safehouse for overseas CIA children. Long-forgotten memories, including a half dozen enumerated in this memoir and others less certain, were stirred up by his comments. The most obvious: How did I possibly get accepted to Cranbrook School in the first place? Second, how did it happen that Hoey himself gave my family an introductory tour of the school? Plus, he called me to his office two times, both sophomore and junior year, "just to talk." Perhaps all the worst students got that attention, but why was I invited to join him for a lavish meal with the Booths, the family that created Cranbrook, before attending a show in

Detroit? Pretty clearly, other Cranbrook students didn't get that treatment.

Another four years passed and I was the guest of Professor William Granara at Harvard University Center for Middle Eastern Studies. Pascal Menoret was giving a talk on his just-published book, *Joyriding in Riyadh: Oil, Urbanism, and Road Revolt.* He mentioned in passing that Aramco was littered with CIA agents in the 1950s and '60s. Interrogation skills, honed by a nearly fifty-year investment career, guided the question I asked him afterward in private. "You know, I was in the Aramco community back then, and I didn't see any evidence of the CIA." Menoret was gracious in answering: of course, a child was not going to be aware of CIA presence, and had I heard of George Rentz, the agency's top man in Aramco? Rentz, as I knew, had headed government affairs and was the primary author of the original *Aramco Handbook*. I found later that he'd also written a history of the Saudi State from 1740 to 1800. These activities were of course a perfect cover: plausible reasons for becoming acquainted with important local people, asking them all sorts of questions, and getting to know their political leanings.

After that conversation, memories of the various occurrences sprinkled throughout this book again flooded into my brain. The preponderance of evidence began to look compelling, plus why was Dad always primarily posted in Ras Tanura? There was one solid contrary argument; Dad had worked long and hard for Aramco. A "spy" would want an easy cover job. Remember Randy Vaughan's friend, the son of a Beirut-based CIA agent mentioned in chapter 16? That man had appeared to be a sales rep for Collins Radio. A perfect cover job—fly everywhere, meet with lots of people, and no one could actually tell what you were doing.

As I thought through all this, there arose in me another source of skepticism—call it the English Lit concern. Tarzan wasn't just a little white child miraculously raised by apes. No, he was Lord Greystoke. Charles Dickens's orphan foundling, Oliver Twist, had rich and powerful grandparents. You get the picture: Was a CIA relationship just my fantasy of importance for the future I'd lost? I kept pulling on the threads of fact and shadow.

In March 2015, after my retirement from Prospector Partners, I traveled to KSA and a Saudi Aramco–sponsored reunion. At the Community Heritage Gallery, I met an informed docent/researcher, who led me to other American Brats of my generation. Many said yes, their fathers had CIA relationships. One, for example, had been a senior officer in the wartime OSS, the forerunner of today's CIA, before he was implanted in Aramco. Eventually my trail of inquiry led to Kai Bird.

Bird, an outstanding Pulitzer Prize–winning author who is five years younger than myself, lived as a youth on the Dhahran air base I'd visited in my days as a Khobar kid. One of his outstanding books, *The Good Spy*, recounted the life of Arabic-speaking CIA officer Robert Ames, who was also on the base back in the day. It was Bird who helped get me to this reasonable conclusion: Dad was not a CIA officer but very likely a CIA asset or agent. The agency likely took advantage of Dad's patriotism and his position. He may have been identified by his original employment application, or possibly at Sidon in December 1954. He was probably cultivated, tested, developed—asked to carry in ammunition, along with other things. They'd know he was a man of action who could and would completely disable a refinery, a skill that had real value, should it be needed. Plus, he was right there and very inexpensive. The cost was some attention and a few favors. My Cranbrook admittance being an obvious example of the latter. Did our family saving 75 percent of pretax Aramco earnings during our years in Arabia mean another source of income? I'm not sure but don't think so. But did the CIA fund the purchase of the VW Microbus that was never picked up in July of 1965? Quite possibly, and it would have been less embarrassing to add those funds to Dad's estate rather than ask for the money back.

Since concluding Dad had CIA involvement, more confirming circumstantial evidence has trickled in. With each National Archives declassification of information, or security breach, we learn ever more about CIA policy and planning. Denying the Russians Middle Eastern oil in the event of war, circa 1955 to 1965, was a priority. We also glimpse the extent to which Aramco and the other big oil producers were involved knowingly and unknowingly in these plans and preparations. Dad was probably only one of the CIA's agents in place in Ras Tanura. It's going to take a powerful lot of evidence to convince me otherwise.*

---

* Those still skeptical might wish to read Steve Everly's June 23, 2016, *Politico Magazine* article: "The Top-Secret Cold War Plan to Keep Soviet Hands Off Middle Eastern Oil."

REFLECTIONS

This is a memoir. It recounts events, reeks of emotion, and contains history, psychology, some geography, and even a touch of geology. The uncharitable might even call it a travelogue. The powers that be (whoever they are) might well prefer that some of its disclosures be lost in the sands of time. It relies on secondhand information, a likely high probability or two, personal experience more than scholarship, and a few intellectual plagiarisms—but to the best of my knowledge it is true. Admittedly, a few "facts" that I thought were true years ago, such as exactly what Florence Chadwick accomplished and just where the Marines landed in Beirut, have been recently adjusted. Plus, I'll admit to deleting the presence and survival of at least two baboons in the cargo hold of PIA Flight 705, based upon literary considerations. They lived and my family perished.

Writing is hard work, and this memoir was no exception. It is painfully personally embarrassing, and thanks only to my retirement and the passing of my own "sell by" date, do I find it fit for publication. It wouldn't have been written were it not for the COVID-19 pandemic. During my quarantine, I reviewed my father's never-touched work journals for the first time. Boxes packed by my parents' friends so long ago, and one packed by Dad in 1957, were finally opened. A torrent of love letters written during the war poured out of the last one. Very little mention of that very same war, other than the terse remark that Dad had helped send a good number of Japanese ships to "Davy Jones's locker" in the last twelve months of the war. Also saved were shooting target bull's-eyes that spoke forcefully of Dad's weapons skill. In one letter he speaks of skeet shooting with a revolver. Apparently, it took an hour or two for him to master using the left hand, and his instructor trained him to have both eyes open, rather than the one-eyed aiming he used with a rifle. Sixty, or even twenty, years ago I'd have been shocked to read the contents of these letters; today nothing surprises me.

In contrast, people who have known me only during the years since the crash may well be surprised at some of what this memoir reveals. My early life has been kept well hidden from most. My sons were nearing adulthood before they and Yvette accidently learned of my twin foster sisters, Eileen and Laurie. Friends and acquaintances may certainly have recognized I was a prisoner to my childhood scars; they just haven't known how many and how deep the wounds were.

People are a complex combination of their experiences and innate underlying personalities. The incidents I've related resonated with me at the time, or I wouldn't have remembered them. Some, like the crash, would resonate with anyone. Others, such as my memories of the Aalsmeer Flower Auction, might not merit a mention in another person's story. It's accepted wisdom that firstborn children with their added responsibilities will be more focused on success in life. I was a firstborn twice. It's accepted wisdom that children who experience devastating reversal of fortune will never stop trying to financially protect those they love. That box was pretty clearly ticked. Did I just happen to "enjoy" the perfect youth to prepare me for a professional investing career? Certainly, but perhaps I was also predisposed to accept those experiences. Let's just agree to watch the nature versus nurture debate in Eddie Murphy's classic movie *Trading Places* with an open mind. As one of my great T. Rowe Price bosses once said, "Whether life grinds you down or polishes you depends on what you're made of." Well, I sure got polished but sadly got ground down a bit as well.

Children and adolescents mature and develop at different rates. Those elementary school classmates I slaughtered playing Chinese checkers so many years ago weren't necessarily stupid. They just hadn't developed an ability to think ahead and anticipate the disruptions an opponent might inflict. Not being able to spell at age fifteen isn't a badge of honor, but it isn't an irrevocable ticket to manual labor either. Sadly, for me, my teachers were focused on reading and spelling, not critical thinking. I forgive them; I never let them convince me I was stupid, no matter how hard they tried. (See, I'm not bitter.) Today our schools seem overrun with specialists aimed at solving learning disabilities. Maybe that's the way to go; I might well have benefited, but I doubt it would have helped much. Regardless, I'd settle for teachers breaking the halo habit. Please stop anticipating that last year's poor student will be this year's poor student, even if almost invariably that's the case. There is reasonable and appropriate public outrage over the stereotyping of races and other groups—the same should apply to poor spellers. (Okay, that was tongue in cheek.) Education, despite my miserable start, ended up being my ticket to a better life. Somewhere, somehow, others will grab that same brass ring. I've tried to repay my debt by serving on two different university trustee boards and by financing about two dozen college educations. Most can't do that, but you can send a few dollars to your alma mater to help the next batch of students.

Not many people can say they lost a family growing up. Early on I lost two foster sisters and had my dad go away for a year; to an eight-year-old, that felt like losing a family. Then, eleven years later, I really lost my family. The first experience might not have the same story appeal or be as interesting or unique, but it hurt, and to some extent prepared me for the second. Regardless, my childhood was largely a happy one, because I loved and was loved in return. To this day memories of my sisters, especially Beth, stir my emotions. My father, in particular, involved me in his affairs probably because they interested me, and I was his logical confidant. I've tried to engage similarly with my own sons, Robert and Paul.

I was also blessed by the fact that Dad recognized our Arabian experience was historic. It was still a medieval land when we arrived, where the huge oil-price gains and production increases were largely unforeseen fifteen years in the future. His identifying "this is the last of the caravans," or "pearling is over" resonated as important to me at the time, and proved prescient. I became a minor

From the moment of Beth's birth, I had vowed to be the best big brother ever ... and I usually came close. This picture was taken moments before I left Saudi Arabia in September of 1964. Losing her was the most devastating experience of my life.

league equivalent of Lloyd Hamilton, at the right place at the right time, even if I was only a bystander. How many preteens in the United States followed the Suez Crisis or the Marines' landing in Lebanon with my focus? How many had the immediate awareness of labor riots or the historic nature of a country's first girls' school? Mine was a role to revel in and learn from.

I have a special affection for other Aramco Brats, with whom I share so much. Our world of sixty-five years ago was unique—the isolation, the unusual mix of people. A world whose limited entertainment options helped initiate my lifelong orgy of reading. It was, of course, an artificial world; a world without the poor or the very rich. A world without old people to care for. A world that excluded 99 percent of Aramco's Saudi employees and their families. A world where, with only a few spectacular exceptions, almost no one died. We Brats were practically the only unproductive inhabitants, and as a result, got way more attention than a normal society would have provided. But don't think it was a perfect world. It attracted men like Dad, who were having a tough time financially and professionally in America, and I suspect it still does. It pains me to remember this, but based on her bruises, a girl in my Ras Tanura class was obviously getting frequent beatings at home. Was her father the only child abuser? What was her, or perhaps her mother's, recourse in a company town?

Has Bratdom changed since I arrived in Arabia on January 2, 1956? Most certainly yes, but perhaps not as much as you might think. True, the jack-of-all-trades American craftsman is no longer. And true, the camps are much more homogeneous, people-wise. But Brats are still a pampered lot—we, *you*, deserve it. Saudi Aramco fathers—yes, almost entirely fathers—are making significantly more money than they would in the States. Many, like the fathers of sixty-five years ago, will be typical nouveau riche in their spending and attitudes. (Sadly, not my personal experience—my dad saved.) Isolation continues, even if the internet connection works consistently, and even if mom and the kiddies fly away for the summer months. Abqaiq and Ras Tanura, in particular, have physically not changed much, although Dhahran has. All three communities are very nice places to live, considerably nicer than the communities just beyond the fence that Dad worked so hard to improve. It remains an artificial world, just not nearly as artificial as it was sixty-five years ago.

Furthermore, Bratdom hasn't changed in one other terribly important respect. Sooner or later, Brats do not have a hometown to go back to. Every two years, on our long vacations, the Howards would head back to Bridgton, Maine, where Dad grew up and his parents, his sisters, and their families, and more than a few high school friends, still lived. Walking down Main Street, seemingly random people would recognize him and stop and chat. Shop clerks and store owners changed only slowly. Friends of his parents' generation were largely unchanged. Brats don't have that experience, and Dad was oblivious to that negative aspect of the situation he had put me in. Were it allowed, I would maintain a small second home in Najmah or at least have a rental and visit every early spring. Saudi Aramco has graciously included older Brats in their employee-retiree reunions, and it's wonderful, but it is just not the same as having a hometown you can always come back to or retire in. It can't be.

Seen from the snug confines of the United States, the outside world appears, and certainly can be, a dangerous place. Flying off to Arabia takes courage. The physical danger was not that great in 1956, but any venture into the unknown requires bravery. For a Brat to go to Arabia, however, does not require a step into the unknown. Perhaps that is why so many have been drawn back to work for the company of their fathers. Despite headline news of Middle Eastern wars or terrorist activities, Brats were, and are, comfortable with the Arabian home they grew up in. They realize that the occasional Scud fragment or the botched Italian bombing raid of World War II were not that dangerous. (The more recent Khobar Towers bombing is another matter altogether.) Regardless, more than one Aramcon of my day did not survive his time in Arabia. My fourth-grade Dhahran classmate and good friend Osama Mikhail lost his forty-four-year-old physician father in a plane crash thirteen months before my family's crash. And a Rome terrorist incident took the lives of twenty-three Aramcons, circa 1970.

Courage is one thing; however, sending your son at age fourteen across the Atlantic to Beirut by himself, or leaving your twenty-three-month-old daughter for a week with strangers, or driving through desolate lands with an eighteen-year-old who can't defend himself, today seems borderline irresponsible. Was I just an added bit of cover for Dad? I'm not all that keen on patriotically risking my life for a few CIA favors, either. Did Dad know he was risking his life? Did he know he was risking mine? Absolutely. How many men write their sons four-page letters, "to be opened in the event of my death?" How many inventory their possessions and check the social security benefits due their wife and daughter before setting out on a trip? Dad did both those things in May 1965, and today my first reaction is that I'm not at all pleased that he wanted to share the dangers of the trip. Upon reflection, however, my eighteen-year-old self might well have been very happy to be a part of his world. Would he have "come clean" with regard to his secret life once we got to Ras

Tanura? Perhaps he was addicted to the stress and wanted me to be proud of him? I suspect so, and I suspect I would have been proud of him.

Sorry, Dad, I love you, but you were playing for big stakes. Did traveling with me behind the Iron Curtain reduce your risk? Was my educational success at Cranbrook just another chip in your career plans? As you rose in Aramco and associated with people at higher levels, did paying for my college seem more important to your career? I'd like to think that your improving financial circumstances were the key, but I'm not sure. You were taking both big and small risks. Some of those put me at risk, some did not, and admittedly the Cranbrook favor you "earned" turned out to be a huge factor in bettering my life. Thanks to a big effort, you could speak, read, and write Arabic and were obviously using Tom Barger as a role model. Had you survived, would a top post at Aramco have been yours? My guess is you would have reached a high level in management. You were the right age, and there would have been few others with your education, compatibility with Saudis, and similar long service. Aramco's reductions in force (RIFs) during the late 1950s had winnowed out many with similar qualifications. Would having a son with a Harvard MBA have helped your career? Certainly, but without the crash, would I have gotten into HBS? I had learned to disguise my spelling problems and had put the struggles of ACS behind me when I entered Millikin, but would I have had the same focus and determination to succeed? I like to think so, but it's hard to tell. Perhaps, like most fathers, you just wanted the best for a son you thought capable.

The CIA connection was at first a career plus, but it kept you in Ras Tanura, away from the Dhahran "flagship" where promotions were more likely. We'll never know what might or would have happened.

History is written by the winners and even more so by the survivors. Perhaps Dad's war experience left him feeling invulnerable; I know the crash left me feeling very vulnerable. I could easily have been on that plane with my family. Why was I spared? In any case, I'm the survivor left to write this story of my youth. It's my story, and also in a very meaningful way, it's my salute to Dad and my family, both then and now, and to the twenty or perhaps forty-plus years that we missed out on spending together.

ACKNOWLEDGMENTS

It is with overwhelming gratitude that I recognize first and foremost the contribution of my book advisor and editor, Mary Norris. My early readers/critics, including Yvette Howard, Timothy Parrish, Patricia Daunic, Paul Howard, and Robert Howard, all deserve special praise for the hours they spent improving the manuscript and its illustrations. Many others contributed facts and insights to my writing effort, including David Wright, Jonathan Cross, Donald Hiser, Randolph Vaughan, Gregory Dearth, Richard Owen, Katie Homewood-Muris, Diana Ryrholm-Geerdes, Thomas Owen, Cynthia Grosch, David Wilson, Arthur Clark, Marianne Hraibi, and Joseph Meadors. All those mentioned gave freely of their knowledge and expertise. *Aramco Brat* is a better book because of them.

ABOUT THE AUTHOR

Rich Howard lives comfortably in Guilford, Connecticut, with his wife, Yvette, and two cats. Close by are his sons, Robert and Paul, their wives, and his five grandchildren. His working past included managing both billion-dollar mutual funds and the similar-sized investment portfolios of institutional clients. He is now trying to become semiretired. However, the supposed occasional hour spent analyzing energy securities continues to engage him and typically leads to far more work. Boiling Point Energy, the small family investment partnership he helps manage, is named for the Ras Tanura home he left so many years ago.

Rich has served on the Board of Trustees of both Millikin University and Quinnipiac University where he is happy to now have emeritus status, having largely reduced responsibilities. Other enjoyed activities include woodworking, gardening, and reading. Thanks to the inactivity caused by COVID-19, he is "probably" retired from playing basketball. *Aramco Brat*, his first book, has taught him that writing is hard work. In the unlikely event he authors a second, it will be an espionage novel that plagiarizes *Brat* and fills in the blanks of what might and may well have happened during his time in Arabia.